The Complete Dublin Diary of Stanislaus Joyce

The Complete Dublin Diary
of Stanislaus Joyce

edited by

GEORGE H. HEALEY

Cornell University Press

ITHACA AND LONDON

PR
6019
.O9
Z6477

This book has been published with the aid of a grant from the Hull Memorial Publication Fund of Cornell University.

The Dublin Diary of Stanislaus Joyce
    first published 1962

The Complete Dublin Diary of Stanislaus Joyce
    first published 1971

Frontispiece: Stanislaus Joyce about 1904

International Standard Book Number 0-8014-0616-1
Library of Congress Catalog Card Number 77-144033

Printed in the United States of America by Vail-Ballou Press, Inc.

Preface

Maurice Daedalus, the brother in James Joyce's *Stephen Hero*, keeps a diary. Mr. Duffy, the principal character of "A Painful Case," in *Dubliners*, likewise keeps "a little sheaf of papers held together with a brass pin," in which "a sentence was inscribed from time to time." Both Maurice Daedalus and Mr. Duffy are derived from the author's younger brother Stanislaus, and Stanislaus did indeed keep a diary, in which the sentences he inscribed from time to time often had to do with his brother. That sheaf of papers, still held together by the brass pin, has survived and is here published in full.

Though called a diary by Stanislaus and James, and hence by others who have mentioned it, the manuscript is rather a collection of descriptions, confessions, anecdotes, and comments. Some are dated, some are not. Some are placed in chronological sequence, some are not. The journal records events in the daily life and thoughts of the tormented young Dubliner who, though uncertain about many things, was utterly convinced even then that his brother was an extraordinary person whose quality the world would one day recognize and whose thoughts and actions were worth setting down. "The interest which I took in Jim's life was the main interest I took in my own; my life is dull without him," he writes in a separate note after James's departure from Ireland. In recording incidents of his own life, then, Stanislaus includes a good deal about James's, at a time when he probably knew his brother better than anyone else did. Since James Joyce conspicuously assumes his readers to be acquainted with minute details of his personal history, Stanislaus' journal is often relevant to James's writings. The diary begins in 1903, soon after the crisis of their mother's death, and ends sometime in 1905, after James's sailing for the Continent has left journal and journalist noticeably less lively. But James is never absent from the diary for long, and throughout much of it he and his doings, at one of the most interesting periods of his life, appear on almost every page. Although Stanislaus gives to no entry the date 16 June—he could hardly have predicted Bloomsday—he does mention in one place or other many of the persons who appear as characters in *Ulysses*, and many also who turn up in *Dubliners*, *Stephen Hero*, and *A Portrait of the Artist as a Young Man*. A large circle of relatives, friends, and acquaintances of the young Joyces are assembled here, Gogarty, Byrne, Cosgrave, the Sheehys, the Murrays, and many another, and also of course the Joyces themselves, of 7 St. Peter's Terrace, Cabra.

That house held small happiness then for anyone, and Stanislaus' picture of the Joyces' home life is likely to rouse both indignation and compassion. James was not much at home in 1904, but Stanislaus had no Martello tower, and the other children were either too small or too enmeshed to escape. Stanislaus gives us here, with a curious mixture of candor, irritation, and affection, a picture—apparently the only picture—of his brothers and sisters. He gives a picture of his father, too, but without affection. Toward John Stanislaus Joyce his second son felt little but contempt, though with some understanding. It is hard to believe that the same man, the same father, stands behind both James's portrayal of Simon Dedalus and Stanislaus' portrayal of "Pappie." The two brothers saw in their wretched surroundings no prospect of betterment and no choice but to endure or to escape. Even their youth, which allowed James some degree of tolerance, hope, and gaiety, offered little compensation to Stanislaus. He seems to have sought relief in writing down his indignations and the indignities that caused them. His testimony in turn stimulated the imagination of James, to whom the "paralysis" of Dublin life had literary uses. James read these minutes while they were being written, asked to have them sent to him after he left Ireland, and borrowed from them the kind of small thing that none but James Joyce would have found worth borrowing at all.

This diary was recorded with great care by a sensitive and intelligent boy, eighteen years old at its opening, twenty at its close, who knew that something was dismally wrong with his life, who reacted by lashing out savagely at almost everything around him, who was often injudicious and unjust, but who was trying to be reasonable and honest. He did not spare others, but neither did he spare himself. He was painfully self-conscious, about his clothes, his manners, his reputation, and even the shape of his head. He recognized his own intelligence but could find nothing to do with it. He abhorred the commonplace, but everything around him, except his brother and his little cousin, appeared to be deadeningly commonplace. His awkward, adolescent tenderness for little Katsy Murray, like everything else, offered him little comfort and less hope. He could not properly be in love with her now: she was too young. He could not properly be in love with her ever, really: she was his first cousin, and marriage to her, in Ireland, would be impossible. His attitude toward his talented brother was already what it was to remain generally throughout their lives, that of unselfish concern for James's comfort, welfare, success, and reputation, sustained in the face of his own wistful longings and James's familiar ingratitude. "But it is terrible to have a cleverer elder brother . . ." (p. 50). Stanislaus, though nearly three years younger than James, was already his brother's whetstone and sometimes his keeper. It was not a comfortable station. He wanted to emulate James but was charged with imitating him. He wanted to share James's life but was repelled by its dissipations. He wanted a place in James's circle of friends but disliked and distrusted most of the persons he met there. James on the other hand found in his younger brother a loyal ally, sympathetic toward his notions and patient of his mockery. From Stanislaus, James borrowed money, clothes, ideas, and traits for the characters in his writings. Maurice Daedalus and Mr. Duffy are obvious enough, but there is more than a little of Stanislaus' envy, pride, and gloom in Stephen himself.

As a physical object the manuscript itself illustrates part of the story it recounts. It consists of 230 pages of writing on sheets cut to about eight by six and a half inches. These sheets, most of them previously used on one side, were culled from old business letters, school exercises, ledger paper, notebook leaves, and similar odds and ends. At least one sheet is a palimpsest; the diarist erased a whole page of something else to gain a usable page for himself. Of some sheets, the writing on the back is not important. Of many, however, it consists of early writings by James, in both verse and prose, that otherwise would have perished. Some of that material, so inadvertently preserved, has been published by Ellsworth Mason and Richard Ellmann in their *Critical Writings of James Joyce*. Stanislaus' text is written neatly, in a tight hand, over every inch of the precious paper. He copied from a draft of some kind, for revisions are rare and he mentions a "Book of Days," which presumably contained his first notes. He calls the collection at various times his "Diary," his "Notes," and his "Crucible." After it was finished, he worked through it and added dates, sometimes in red pencil, in the margins. These dates, be it noted, refer not to the time of the writing but rather to the time of the incident itself. The pagination of the manuscript indicates that the text was intended to stand in its present order. The dates were considered to be incidental and in several instances are out of sequence.

This diary was preceded by one covering two years that was deliberately destroyed in 1903, the year this one begins. Stanislaus in his writings and correspondence quotes, from what he calls "my diary," material of 1904 that is not found in this manuscript. Such material may have come from the few leaves now missing from the sheaf or more likely from some other document not now with his papers at Cornell. He used the diary here published in preparing the autobiographical *My Brother's Keeper*, but the two do not much overlap. *My Brother's Keeper*, which he did not live to finish, brings the story to about the time of the mother's death in August 1903. This diary begins a few weeks after that event and carries on for about a year and a half. Stanislaus' diary is often callow when compared to *My Brother's Keeper*, but it is nearer Dublin by fifty years, and what it lacks in sophistication it may gain in immediacy.

Young Stanislaus' punctuation was erratic and his spelling, especially of proper names, uncertain. Both have sometimes been modified for the convenience of the reader. Together with the marginal dates, the diarist also added a number of glosses that correct, criticize, or extend his original remarks. Most of these glosses seem to be contemporary with the original, but since they cannot be dated with certainty they are carried separately and identified as "MS notes."

This edition gives the complete text of the manuscript. An earlier edition entitled *The Dublin Diary of Stanislaus Joyce*, published in 1962, omitted certain parts of the diary for a number of unrelated reasons. Some of the material then set aside would have embarrassed persons then living, some would have strained the tolerance of publishers and public, some was thought to hold only marginal interest because of having little to do with James Joyce. The passage of time has now removed or modified most of the solicitudes of a decade ago, and Stanislaus' emergence as a person interesting in his own right has liberated his diary from depending wholly on his brother for its interest. Everything now present in the diary, including about thirty-six pages of manuscript not printed in the first edition, appears here. Ellipses and dashes, where they occur, are transcribed from the source. A few errors in the earlier edition have been corrected, and, thanks in part to advances in Joyce scholarship during the interval, the explanatory notes have been revised and extended. The editor thanks the Cornell University Library Board for permission to publish the manuscript.

G. H. H.

Ithaca, New York
January 1971

Contents

The Complete Dublin Diary
of Stanislaus Joyce

Jim's character is unsettled; it is developing. New influences are coming over him daily, he is beginning new practices. He has come home drunk three or four times within the last month (on one occasion he came home sick and dirty-looking on Sunday morning, having been out all night) and he is engaged at present in sampling wines and liqueurs and at procuring for himself the means of living. He has or seems to have taken a liking for conviviality, even with those whose jealousy and ill-will towards himself he well knows, staying with them a whole night long dancing and singing and making speeches and laughing and reciting, and revelling in the same manner all the way home. To say what is really his character, one must go beneath much that is passing in these influences and habits and see what it is in them that his mind really affects; one must compare what he is with what he was, one must analyse, one must judge him by his moments of exaltation, not by his hours of abasement.[1]

1. Written across this paragraph is the word 'rubbish'.

His intellect is precise and subtle, but not comprehensive. He is no student. His artistic sympathy and judgment are such as would be expected in one of his kind of intellect—if he were not more than a critic, I believe, he would be as good a critic of what interests him as any using English today. His literary talent seems to be very great indeed, both in prose and in verse.[2] He has, as Yeats says, a power of very delicate spiritual writing and whether he writes in sorrow or is young and virginal, or whether (as in 'He travels after the wintry sun')[3] he writes of what he has seen, the form is always either strong, expressive, graceful or engaging, and his imagination open-eyed and classic. His 'epiphanies'—his prose pieces (which I almost prefer to his lyrics) and his dialogues—are again subtle. He has put himself into these with singular courage, singular memory, and scientific minuteness; he has proved himself capable of taking very great pains to create a very little thing of prose or verse. The keen observation and satanic irony of his character are precisely, but not fully, expressed. Whether he will ever build up anything broad—a drama, an esthetic treatise—I cannot say. His genius is not literary and he will probably run through many of the smaller forms of literary artistic expression. He has made living his end in life, and in the light of this magnificent importance of living, everything else is like a rushlight in the sun. And so he is more interested in the sampling of

2. MS note: 'He is not an artist he says. He is interesting himself in politics—in which he says [he has] original ideas. He says he does not care for art or music though he admits he can judge them. He lives on the excitement of incident.'

3. From 'Tilly', published in *Pomes Penyeach*.

liqueurs, the devising of dinners, the care of dress, and whoring, than to know if the one-act play—'the dwarf-drama' he calls it—is an artistic possibility.

Jim is a genius of character. When I say 'genius', I say just the least little bit in the world more than I believe; yet remembering his youth and that I sleep with him, I say it. Scientists have been called great scientists because they have measured the distances of the unseen stars, and yet scientists who have watched the movements in matter scarcely perceptible to the mechanically aided senses have been esteemed as great; and Jim is, perhaps, a genius though his mind is minutely analytic. He has, above all, a proud, wilful, vicious selfishness, out of which by times now he writes a poem or an epiphany, now commits the meannesses of whim and appetite, which was at first protestant egoism, and had, perhaps, some desperateness in it, but which is now well-rooted—or developed?—in his nature, a very Yggdrasill.[4] He has extraordinary moral courage—courage so great that I have hopes that he will one day become the Rousseau of Ireland. Rousseau, indeed, might be accused of cherishing the secret hope of turning away the anger of disapproving readers by confessing unto them, but Jim cannot be suspected of this. His great passion is a fierce scorn of what he calls the 'rabblement'—a tiger-like, insatiable hatred. He has a distinguished appearance and bearing and many graces: a musical singing and especially speaking voice (a tenor), a good undeveloped talent in music, and witty conversation. He has a distressing habit of saying quietly to those with whom he is familiar the most

4. The great ash tree symbolic of the universe in Norse mythology.

shocking things about himself and others, and, moreover, of selecting the most shocking times, saying them, not because they are shocking merely, but because they are true. They are such things that even knowing him well as I do, I do not believe it is beyond his power to shock me or Gogarty [5] with all his obscene rhymes. His manner however is generally very engaging and courteous with strangers, but, though he dislikes greatly to be rude, I think there is little courtesy in his nature. As he sits on the hearth-rug, his arms embracing his knees, his head thrown a little back, his hair brushed up straight off his forehead, his long face red as an Indian's in the reflexion of the fire, there is a look of cruelty in his face. Not that he is not gentle at times, for he can be kind, and one is not surprised to find simpleness in him. (He is always simple and open with those that are so with him.) But few people will love him, I think, in spite of his graces and his genius, and whosoever exchanges kindnesses with him is likely to get the worst of the bargain. (This is coloured too highly, like a penny cartoon.)

[26 September 1903]

Jim says it is not moral courage in him but as he phrases it of himself, 'when the Bard begins to write he intellectualizes himself.' Jim's voice, when in good form, has a beautiful flavour, rich and pure, and goes through one like a strong exhilarating wine. He sings well.

5. Oliver St. John Gogarty, the original of Buck Mulligan in *Ulysses*.

Jim has a wolf-like intellect, neither massive nor very strong, but lean and ravenous, tearing the heart out of his subject.

Pappie [1] is very scurrilous.

He scourges the house with his tongue.

Mother kept the house together at the cost of her life.[2]

The Sophists will never be extinct while Jim is alive.

The twelve tribes of Galway are:

Athy, Blake, Bodkin
Deane, D'Arcy, Lynch
Joyce, Kirwin, Martin
Morris, Skerret, French

Pappie is the only child of an only child (his father) and therefore the spoiled son of a spoiled son, the spendthrift son of a spendthrift. His temperament was probably Gasconish—gallant and sentimental—and was certainly shallow and without love. If he ever had any self-criticism his inordinate self-love and vanity choked it in his early youth. Yet, strangely enough, he is shrewd in his judgment of others. He takes pride in a family of some refinement, education and some little distinction on one side, and of some wealth on the other. He is domineering and quarrelsome and has in an unusual degree that low, voluble abusiveness characteristic of the Cork people when drunk. He is worse in this respect since we have grown up because even when silent we are an opposition. He is ease-loving and his ambition in life has been to be respected and to keep up appearances. However unworthy this may sound, it has been so difficult of attainment and he has struggled for it

1. John S. Joyce, father of the author.
2. Mrs. May Joyce had died on 13 August 1903, at the age of 44.

with such tenacious energy against the effects of his constant drunkenness that it is hard to despise it utterly. He is lying and hypocritical. He regards himself as the victim of circumstances and pays himself with words. His will is dissipated, and his intellect besotted, and he has become a crazy drunkard. He is spiteful like all drunkards who are thwarted, and invents the most cowardly insults that a scandalous mind and a naturally derisive tongue can suggest. He undoubtedly hastened Mother's death. He was an insulting son, and as a husband, a household bully and a bester in money matters. For his children he has no love or care but a peculiar sense of duty arising out of his worship of respectability. He is full of prejudices, which he tries to instil into us, regarding all opposition as impertinent puppyism. He boasts of being a bit of a snob. His idea of the home is a well-furnished house in which he can entertain and his children grow up under their mother's care, and to which, having spent the evening in drinking and story-telling with his friends, he can return to lord it and be obeyed.

He is generous, however, and when he claims to have 'some ideas of a gentleman' he does not seem to be ridiculous. When he has been sober for a few days he is strangely quiet, though irritable and nerve-shaken, with a flow of lively talk. It is difficult to talk to him even now at 54 for his vanity is easily hurt. Moreover this quietness seems unnatural and to be the reaction of his drunkenness.

He has the remains of the best tenor of the light English style I ever heard. His range was unusual and he sings with taste.

Jim's ingenuousness and gentleness are false, and since

I pointed this out to him his affectation of false ingenuousness and false gentleness has been false.

I see in his verse and prose self-deception and a desire for display without the redeeming foolishness of vanity.

Jim claims of his friends the right to ruin himself.

Jim has a hardly controlled itch for deceit. He lies without reason and exerts himself to deceive those that know him best, from a contempt of the dullness of morality and right-doing.

When Pappie is sober and fairly comfortable he is easy and pleasant spoken though inclined to sigh and complain and do nothing. His conversation is reminiscent and humourous, ridiculing without malice, and accepting peace as an item of comfort. This phase is regrettably rare and of short duration. It comes at times of dire poverty and does not last till bedtime. The mood is genuine, indeed, but a chance phrase will reveal that it is more an amnesty temporarily agreed to than a peace. Unsettling from his comfortable position before the fire and gathering up his papers to go to bed effect a change in him, and he goes up the stairs complaining and promising changes over which he has no control.

Pappie has for many years regarded his family as an encumbrance which he suffers impatiently while he must, and which he seeks to cast off at the earliest opportunity. Jim and I and Charlie,[3] who naturally do not see matters in this light, he abuses and threatens as wasters. He calls all his children bastards as a habit, and really the treatment he wishes to give them is that enforced by law even to bastards—support until the sixteenth year for a male child.

3. Charles, then 17, was the youngest of the surviving brothers.

He is truculent and inflicts a thoughtless selfishness on his children. I have said he has a peculiar sense of duty toward them. It is true, but that sense does not include the office of feeding them regularly. Even tonight when his being was comfortable there was a somewhat vicious hue about his contentment.

My cousin Kathleen Murray (called Katsy) [4] has a luxurious nature and the promise of a magnificent contralto. It has the depth (in tone) of a bass and I flattered myself that I first discovered it in her.

That amongst his innumerable acquaintances, Pappie had a few real friends, is to be remembered to his credit.

At that time which I remember most vividly, Mother had little left of what had once made her a figure in drawing-rooms, little except a very graceful carriage and occasional brilliancy at the piano. She had a small, very feminine head, and was pretty. I remember her intelligent, sparing, very patient in troubles (the normal state) and too patient of insults. When I saw her lying in her brown habit on the bed in the front room, her head a little wearily to one side, I seemed to be standing beside the death-bed of a victim. Now for the first time waking in the quietness and subdued light of the room, beside the candles and the flowers, she had the importance that should always have been hers. An ever-watchful anxiety for her children, a readiness to sacrifice herself to them utterly, and a tenacious energy to

4. Though only about 14 years of age, Katsy Murray had previously attracted the passing interest of James and was now receiving the shy attentions of Stanislaus. Her mother (Aunt Josephine) was a favorite of the Joyce boys. Her father (Uncle Willie), brother of Mrs. Joyce, is the Richie Goulding of *Ulysses*.

endure for their sakes replaced love in a family not given to shows of affection. She was very gentle towards her children though she understood them each. It is understanding and not love that makes the confidence between Mother and children so natural though unacknowledged, so unreserved though nothing is confessed (there is no need of words or looks between them, the confidence surrounds them like the atmosphere). Rather it is this understanding that makes the love so enduring. Pappie, who had no relatives and was free and selfish, demanded of Mother, who had many, alienation from them. I can well believe that she never brought them to his house and that Pappie himself, being weak and inconstant, did; but in heart she was never altogether alienated from them. To have been so for Pappie's sake would have demanded more passionateness than was in Mother's nature. Perhaps if she had done so she would have been just as unloved by one so eminently selfish as Pappie, or if not as unloved certainly as cruelly treated. It is in her favour that in the middle of worries in which it is hard to remain gentle or beautiful or noble Mother's character was refined as much as Pappie's was debased, and she gained a little wisdom. Yet I cannot regard Mother and Pappie as ill-matched, for with Pappie Mother had more than mere Christian patience, seeing in him what only lately and with great difficulty I have seen in him. It is strange, too, that the true friendships Pappie made (with Mr. Kelly [5] for instance) were confirmed at home and, I think, under Mother's influence, his friends being scarcely less friendly towards Mother than towards himself. Up to

5. John Kelly, of Tralee, the John Casey of *A Portrait of the Artist as a Young Man.*

9

the last Mother had a lively sense of humour and was an excellent mimic of certain people. Though worn and grave, Mother was capable at unusual times of unusual energy. She was a selfish drunkard's unselfish wife.

Mother had seventeen children of whom nine are now living.[6]

Mother's treatment of Poppie was unjust, not nearly so unjust but of the same kind as Pappie's treatment of her, and perhaps due a little unconsciously to that example. These women of Nirvana who accept their greatest trials with resignation, letting worries be heaped like ashes on their heads, and hoping only in one thing—their power to live them down, vent themselves in irritability about ridiculous little annoyances. One of the most difficult things to excuse is a nagging temper, but it must be remembered that Mother's temper was only lately of this kind, that it was due to disease in one who died of cirrhosis[7] of the liver, and that it was directed against Poppie from a habit begun when Poppie was young and very obstinate. Mother, too, saw that the reading of life in our home was unchristian and, constantly, deceived herself to make her life submissive to that Priest-worship in which she was reared. She even asserted her Catholicism that by speaking much she might convince herself, and this is called insincerity. Mother's religion was acquiescence and she had the eye of unbelievers constantly upon her.

Jim has lately become a prig about women, affecting to

6. James, b. 1882; Margaret ('Poppie'), b. 1884; Stanislaus, b. 1884; Charles, b. 1886; Eileen, b. 1889; Mary ('May'), b. 1890; Eva, b. 1891; Florence ('Florrie'), b. 1892; and Mabel ('Baby'), b. 1893, George, b. 1887, had died in 1902.

7. The author first wrote 'cancer', but later corrected it.

regard them as dirty animals and frequently quoting an epigram of a **Dr. Perse's.**[8]

Katsy Murray is a type of what the mediaeval schoolmen called 'the pride of the flesh'.

The Murrays don't know the value of kisses.

[*2 February 1904*] [1]

2nd February: 1904: Tuesday. Jim's birthday. He is twenty-two [to]day. He was up late and did not stir out all day, having a bad cold. He has decided to turn his paper [2] into a novel, and having come to that decision is just as glad, he says, that it was rejected. The paper . . . was rejected by the editors, Fred Ryan and W. Magee ('John Eglinton') [3] because of the sexual experiences narrated in it. Jim thinks that they rejected it because it is all about himself, though they professed great admiration for the style of the paper. They always admire his style. Magee has an antipathy for Jim's character, I think. Magee is a dwarfish, brown-clad fellow, with red-brown eyes like a ferret, who walks with his hands in his jacket pockets and

8. MS note: 'Woman is an animal that micturates once a day, defecates once a week, menstruates once a month, and parturates once a year.'

1. The entries under this date do not appear in the Cornell MS (but compare n. 3, p. 20). They were reported by Stanislaus in a letter to a correspondent as being copied from a diary, and they are reprinted here, with the kind permission of Professor Richard Ellmann from his *James Joyce* (New York: Oxford University Press, 1959), pp. 152–153.

2. Entitled 'A Portrait of the Artist'.

3. Ryan and Magee were the editors of *Dana*.

as stiffly as if his knees were roped up with sugauns.[4] He is sub-librarian in Kildare Street, and I think his mission in Ireland is to prove to his Protestant grand-aunts that un-believers can be very moral and admire the Bible. He is interested in great thoughts and philosophy, whenever he can understand it. Jim is beginning his novel, as he usually begins things, half in anger, to show that in writing about himself he has a subject of more interest than their aimless discussion. I suggested the title of the paper 'A Portrait of the Artist', and this evening, sitting in the kitchen, Jim told me his idea for the novel. It is to be almost autobiographi-cal, and naturally as it comes from Jim, satirical. He is putting a large number of his acquaintances into it, and those Jesuits whom he has known. I don't think they will like themselves in it. He has not decided on a title, and again I made most of the suggestions. Finally a title of mine was accepted: 'Stephen Hero,' from Jim's own name in the book 'Stephen Dedalus'. The title, like the book, is satirical. Between us we rechristened the characters, calling them by names which seemed to suit their tempers or which sug-gested the part of the country from which they come. Afterwards I parodied many of the names: Jim, 'Stuck-up Stephen'; Pappie, 'Sighing Simon'; myself, 'Morose Mau-rice'; the sister, 'Imbecile Isabel'; Aunt Josephine (Aunt Bridget), 'Blundering Biddy'; Uncle Willie, 'Jealous Jim.'

Pappie came in very drunk, and—an unusual thing for him—went straight up to bed. Today we have had a grand dinner and tea. It rained heavily after dark. We spent the evening playing cards—in honour of the occasion—Jim

4. Ellmann's note: 'Hay ropes (Irish)'.

and Charlie smoking. Jim wanted to ask Pappie to come down but it was thought better to let him sleep.

The younger Miss Nolan wears her hair very tastefully in an old-fashioned style, parted in the centre and combed flat down. It is black and hangs in a plat behind. She is pretty and looks like as if she stepped out of a Cruikshank illustration to Dickens. I have nick-named her 'Dora'.

Mary Sheehy [1] has a very pleasant speaking voice and an engaging laugh. She seems to be happy and lazy and is often amused. Under her quietness I think she has a merry disposition. She is very handsome and wears an immense plait of soft black hair.

The Irish are represented as being very much afraid of the satire of the wandering poets. This 'satire' is really a habit of nicknaming very prevalent in this country. Scarcely any escape. Among those I know, for instance, Pappie calls Uncle John [2] 'the cornet player' and his wife 'Amina' and 'La Somnambula', William Field [3] 'Hamlet'. Gogarty calls O'Leary Curtis [4] 'the Japanese Jesus', Jim

1. Mary Sheehy, later Mrs. Thomas Kettle, was the first girl, according to Stanislaus, in whom James took an emotional interest.

2. John Murray, brother of Mrs. Joyce, is the Red Murray of the 'Aeolus' episode of *Ulysses*. In the 'Wandering Rocks' episode, Simon Dedalus speaks of 'your uncle John the cornetplayer'.

3. Blackrock butcher and M.P. He appears in the 'Nestor' episode of *Ulysses*.

4. Curtis, a newspaper man, is mentioned in James Joyce's *Gas from a Burner*. He is the O'Madden Burke of 'The Mother' in *Dubliners* and of the 'Aeolus' episode in *Ulysses*.

'Kinch', me 'Thug', Æ 'Corpse-face'. Jim calls 'John Eglinton'[5] 'the horrible virgin.' Pappie calls Aunt Josephine 'the
seal', 'Aunt Hobblesides'. Mother used to call Mr. Richard
Thornton[6] (an amusing, robust, florid little elderly man)
'the dicky bird'. I call Gogarty 'Doll' because he reminds
me of an India-rubber doll, and a young fellow named
Kelly, who goes to Sheehy's, a squat, swarthy chap, 'Frog-
face'.

My sister Eva[7] reminds me of the 'Marchioness' in *The
Old Curiosity Shop*.

Jim says he is not an artist. I think he lives on the excitement of events.

[*29 February 1904*]

The wise virgins delight in the society of the necessitous
young genius. They are happy when he comes in. They
laugh at him, or with him, or for him, making the heart of
the dullard envious. And he is suspected of wild ways.
They flatter him with pressing attention, an interest which
is almost a wish—lasting the whole length of an evening—
to protect him from himself, and which the secret, shy admiration in their eyes—for it is evident they suspect something they slyly will not even with a look question—be-

5. Pseudonym of W. K. Magee, editor, essayist, and poet, of the
staff of the National Library. He appears in *Ulysses*.

6. Thornton, a professional teataster, was a model for Tom
Kernan, who appears in *Ulysses* and in the story 'Grace', in *Dubliners*.

7. Eva, age 12, was the fourth daughter of the family.

trays. There is smiling unacknowledged friendship between them, but no more. They will not meet him on the highways alone, nor will they marry him.[1]

What is the ambition of the hero's valet?

It is most important that I should remember that Pappie is my father. This does not make me think him any different from what he is, but it shows me why I find quite natural to tolerate from him what I would certainly not tolerate from any other.

Jim says he has an instinct for women. He scarcely ever talks decently of them, even of those he likes. He talks of them as of warm, soft-skinned animals. 'That one'd give you a great push.' 'She's very warm between the thighs, I fancy.' 'She has great action, I'm sure.'

Charlie is an absurd creature. He is foolish, a vain and stupid boaster and very sentimental, and has a habit of imitating people he knows. He likes to hear himself talk big and, like his kind, thinks himself shrewd. He is lively and talkative, though rather stupid. He is courageous, too, and against authority spirited. He is an amusing clown when boisterous but rough and loud-voiced, being round-shouldered and awkward and naturally very strong. Yet he has the gift of silence when he likes. I fancy it was kicked into him when he was young for he was treated the worst, being considered an *omadhaun*.[2] He has the gift of writing though practically uneducated, and writes verse. He occasionally expresses himself well, gets a musical effect or a graceful phrase, but is possessed by a love of grandiloquence. One can see by him that he, too, is troubled by that familiar, Self-consciousness, which keeps constantly

1. This paragraph is deleted in the MS.   2. A simpleton.

telling us what we have done and why we did it, and which does not flatter. All of us have this familiar—mine is a me-tormenting 'horla'[3]—and it induces in us a manner which our relatives mistake for pride in us. Charlie is tall for his age (17) and good-looking, small-featured with very thick black hair and wears glasses for a slight turn in his eyes (he is very like a smaller Yeats). But like most of those who are not clever and have been ill-treated he is obstinate and overbearing where he has power. I do not think he has any taste for music though as a boy he had an exceptionally good treble. He drinks, smokes and has whored a little, but he is a Roman Catholic. I do not think he would be a good fellow for a woman to marry.

Besides family feeling and brotherly friendship, Charlie loved Georgie,[4]—far better than any one else in the house.

Georgie was very handsome—very like Jim but with larger and better features. He was a regular young pagan with a very high colour and a brownish skin, and had beau-tiful long hands. He was little over the average height, but nimble and always very neat in his dress though shabby. He was brilliantly selfish and mischievous and had a loud rippling laugh—a Homeric laugh. He was very clever and delicate, excitable and cowardly. He took Jim very seri-ously, and, I think, was beginning to be a pagan in more than nature. The priest who attended him in his last illness was very much attracted by him and said he had an extra-ordinary mind for a boy. He was given a public funeral from Belvedere College where he was a favourite (the only one I remember for 10 years). He was not in the

3. He refers to 'Le Horla', a story by Guy de Maupassant.
4. The youngest son of the family, who had died in March 1902 at the age of 14. James named his son after this brother.

least sentimental and was unemotional. Silence became him very well, and he was often very quiet. He was a most inspiring listener, and had a slight excitable stutter. Jim used to speak to him freely because he was sure of getting intelligence and, under his ridicule, real admiration. He died in his fifteenth year of typhoid badly treated by a stupid doctor. Pappie used to call him 'the Nipper'. Our relatives did not like him.

Pappie had no affection for him.

I was very much attached to him though not so much as Charlie, who was his constant companion. He was the youngest—the cadet.[5]

Jim is often silly-mannered and impolite. I have no doubt that he is a poet, a lyric poet, that he has a still greater mastery of prose. He may be a genius—it seems to me very possible—but that he has not yet found himself is obvious.

The house is and always has been intolerable with bickering, quarrelling and scurrillity. A blaze of a row is almost a relief.

Aunt Josephine, Uncle Willie and their household are very kind to Jim. I do not visit there for I have a prejudice that Uncle Willie's friendship is uncertain.

[*10 January 1904*]

May [1] is a comfortable fat girl, slow and rather chuffy. She does nothing or practically nothing in the house and

5. MS note: 'I know Charlie better lately and I suspect that there was a great deal of sentimental maudlinness in Charlie's affection. Probably, as usual, what affection Jim had was purest.'

1. May, nearing 14, was the third daughter.

will not be forced to do anything but some light and pleasant labour. She used to watch in the room with Mother, who liked to have her there. She is very sensible and has an observant sense of humour. She has no voice but likes music and is clever at it. Eileen amuses her. Of all the girls she is the only one who has any intellectual curiosity. I do not think she will remain a Catholic, for she does not seem to have much religion in her, knows her own mind, and has moreover stubborn courage. She does not look upon priests with any different eyes than those with which she looks upon, say, Pappie's friends or Pappie's self. She once described a certain priest to me as 'don't ye know— a fat chap with queer eyes', and then began to laugh. I like her.

Eileen [2] is older than May. She is very pale, with an expressionless face and thin and fair hair. She would be considered pretty. She is not clever but her manner is very quick and she is inimitably funny, even witty. She works very hard in the house and seems to like it, as she is strong and healthy. She has a good tuneful contralto but no taste for music.[3] She is thoughtless and careless and a greater favourite than May with those that know her. She very rarely laughs, generally keeping an expressionless face and making others laugh. When she laughs she has a contralto's laugh. She dances lightly.

Poppie is a woman, and has a woman's attractiveness, a

2. Eileen, nearly 15, was the second daughter.
3. MS note: 'Eileen's voice is, I believe, becoming very fine and developing into a high soprano. Pappie thinks that as his voice first promised to be a contralto and had depth, that Eileen will be able to make something of it.'

beautiful voice but small when she sings, beautiful eyes, and peculiarly feminine ways. She has stepped into Mother's place, and though uneducated and not over-intelligent she is managing by herself to settle her younger sisters in convents. Pappie gives her no help, but abuse. Among her duties she accepts that of making the younger children speak respectfully of Pappie, and her arguments to this end are *charming* [4] in their inadequacy. She likes music but is not clever at it. She has a good and strange to say strong touch on the piano. She has learnt that Jim and Charlie whore.

Jim is fickle.

Charlie is going on the stage. Engagement off.

[*29 March 1904*]

I suggested the title of a paper of Jim's which was commissioned for a new review to be called *Dana* in February last. It is now almost April and the review has not yet appeared. [1] The paper—the title of which was 'A Portrait of the Artist'—was rejected by the editors Magee ('John Eglinton') and F. Ryan [2] because of the sexual experiences narrated therein—at least this was the one reason they gave. Jim has turned the paper into a novel the title of which— 'Stephen Hero'—I also suggested. He has written eleven

4. MS note: 'Ugh! What a word! Goethe fished it up somewhere when he tried to turn the world into a mutual admiration society. I mean "funny".'

1. The first issue of *Dana* appeared in May.

2. Frederick Ryan was also secretary of the Irish Theatre Society.

chapters. The chapters are exceptionally well written in a style which seems to me altogether original. It is a lying autobiography and a raking satire. He is putting nearly all his acquaintances in it, and the Catholic Church comes in for a bad quarter of an hour. I suggested many of the names for the characters on an onomatopoeic principle.[3]

Anything I owe to Jim I owe to his example, for he is not an encouraging person in criticism. He told me when I began keeping a diary that I would never write prose and that my diary was most uninteresting except in the parts that were about him. (Indeed it was a journal of his life with detailed conversations with him and between him and Irish men of letters, poets, etc., covering often 3 and 4 pages of close-written foolscap. I burnt it to make a holocaust. Perhaps Jim owes something of his appearance to this mirror held constantly up to him. He has used me, I fancy, as a butcher uses his steel to sharpen his knife.) [4] He told me I reminded him of Gogarty's description of Magee, 'that he had to fart every time before he could think', has written an epiphany of a sluggish polar bear on me,[5] and used to say frequently that I was a 'thick-headed bloody fool', even a 'commonplace youth'. He has told me when I am listening seriously to what he is telling 'to please turn my face away as it bored him'. One night when I was ly-

3. MS note: 'I parodied some of the names: Pappie, "Sighing Simon"; Jim, "Stuck-up Stephen"; myself, "Morose Maurice"; the sister, "Imbecile Isabel"; Aunt Josephine (Aunt Brigid), "Blundering Brigid"; Uncle Willie (Uncle Jim), "Jealous Jim".'
4. 'Where is your brother? Apothecaries' hall. My whetstone' (*Ulysses*, New York: Random House, 1934, p. 208).
5. See 'The white mist is falling in slow flakes,' in *Epiphanies*, ed. O. A. Silverman (Buffalo, N.Y.: University of Buffalo, 1956).

ing on my back in bed thinking of something or another, Jim, who was watching me from his, said, 'I wouldn't like to be a woman and wake up to find your "goo" (face) on the pillow beside me in the morning.' Lately he has told me I have a right idea of writing prose and compared my method with his when he was young, laughing at his own. He has also told me that he thought I was wittier than Wilde. Before I believed him because he was telling me my opinion of myself; now I cannot trust his judgment. He also told me my voice was unpleasant and expressionless, though many like it very much. No one whose judgment I respect has told me he liked it, and I cannot help believing Jim as my voice tires my throat and bores me. Christ hear us, Christ graciously hear us.

Jim reconciled his admiration of Italians and his contempt for Rossetti by calling Rossetti an ice-cream Italian.

I called Mr. Kane 'the Green Street Shakespeare'. [6]

It is annoying that I should have a typically Irish head; not the baboon-faced type, but the large, square, low-fronted head of O'Connell, and Curran.

Jim seems to have many friends amongst the younger men he has met.

Charlie's Catholicism is intolerable. He is the spoiled priest to his finger tips. His talk is all of Father This-body and Father That, and this Church and that Church, what he said to the Missioner and how the people were all looking on. He likes to hear himself criticising priests. Of devotional exercises he talks dogmatically like one who knows

6. Matthew Kane, clerk in the Crown Solicitor's office, was the model for Martin Cunningham of *Ulysses* and *Dubliners*. Kane was thought to look like Shakespeare.

all the tricks of the trade. Fr. Brennan [7] is his latest model. He puffs like him when speaking.

To May (whom, by her own account, he bores), 'Oh you know' (puff) 'you can make the seven visits without going any further than Phibsboro here' (puff), 'without going to a single other chapel' (puff). 'But, of course, you're supposed to go to seven chapels if you can' (puff). 'Now today, for instance' (puff), 'I went etc.' I took my candle and went upstairs to bed.

> 'Poet Kinch has a brother called Thug,
> His imitator, and jackal, and mug.
> His stride like a lord's is
> His pretension absurd is
> In fact, he's an *awful* thick-lug.'

Dick Sheehy [8] is a regular Dick—the big, footballing brother.

I am of that temperament which does not decide in its own case.

J. F. Byrne's [9] judgments of people are prejudiced by his desire to accuse.

Jim has the first character of the hero—strange to say, he is noble; and the first character of the lyric poet—he is most susceptible. His affairs have the proper air of reality. His second last was his cousin Katsy Murray—a child. His present Mary Sheehy.

7. Probably Fr. Joseph Brennan of St. Joseph's, Dublin.

8. Of the young members of the hospitable Sheehy family, Richard was closest to James Joyce.

9. J. F. Byrne, in some ways James Joyce's closest friend, is Cranly in *A Portrait of the Artist.*

Mary Sheehy is good looking but ungraceful in figure, and has a beautiful voice. She is romantic but clever and sensible and therefore dissatisfied. She wants Hero.

Mrs. Sheehy-Skeffington (*née* Hannah Sheehy) [10] was till about 27 a student—yet I think she has no sympathy with student life, and does not understand those disattached personalities, the world's poets and artists and cranks, the Shakespeares and the Rimbauds. She is a practical animal and regards as worthless those who do not work, seeing truly enough that men of that stamp will not serve the purpose of her and her kind.

Some names fill me with a strange and troubled pleasure.

A medical student by name Sheehan [11] (an oval-faced, under-shod fellow with a small curly head like an Assyrian king) should be given a civil list pension for a word with which he has enriched the vocabulary—Aquacity.[12] He applied it to obvious statements and to platitudes.

[*12 April 1904*]

I loathe my father. I loathe him because he is himself, and I loathe him because he is Irish—*Irish*, that word that epitomises all that is loathsome to me. I loathe him more than I loathe my Uncle John. He went out today to a funeral at 8.30 and came

10. Wife of Francis Skeffington, who upon his marriage changed his name to include that of his wife.

11. Daniel T. Sheehan, of University College.

12. James Joyce remembered Sheehan's coined word and used it, though with a different meaning, in *Ulysses* (New York: Random House, 1934, p. 657).

[Two leaves are lacking in the manuscript.]

with a pupil scarcely distinct from the iris in a clear white fruit-like ball and a long well-defined eyebrow, an eye Velasquez would have painted.

Jim says Mary Sheehy seems to him like a person who had a great contempt for many of the people she knew. He has written two poems under her inspiration [1] but she is ignorant of his tributes.

I called J. F. Byrne 'the intense face'.

[29 *March 1904*]

We—Jim, Charlie and I—relieve one another in the house like policemen as the girls are not safe in it with Pappie. A few nights ago, not knowing I was in—I do most of the duty—he attempted to strike some of them. He catches at the thing nearest to hand—a poker, plate, cup or pan—to fling at them. This has been the cause of many rows here. If the children see two of us preparing to go out, they run up to the third to ask him to stay in. Last night when I came home from the concert—to go to which by the bye I had to sell a book and borrow

[A leaf is lacking in the manuscript.]

He asked her was she little Miss Joyce, told [her] to tell her father that Mr. Kettle called. 'You won't forget now— Mr. Kettle—what you boil water in.' Baby [1] was telling this as a joke, and Eva, [who] was sitting on the fender at

1. 'What counsel has the learned moon' and 'Lightly come and lightly go'; both were later published in *Chamber Music*.
1. Mabel, age 10, the youngest child.

24

the fire boiling water, said, 'Unfortunately he didn't know that it's Mr. Teapot we boil the water in.' We have no kettle.

[*10 April 1904*]

Gogarty is treacherous in his friendship towards Jim. While never losing an opportunity of 'keeping in touch' with celebrities to whom he is introduced, he affects to care nothing for them, or his own reputation, or anyone else's. He affects to be careless of all things and carries this out by acting generously towards Jim in regard to money. The other day Yeats, Ryan, Colum and Gogarty [were] talking and Yeats mentioned a fellow in London who was making three hundred a year writing short clever articles for some London paper. 'It is a pity Joyce couldn't get something like that,' said Ryan. 'He could write the articles all right, but then he couldn't keep sober for three days together.' 'Why put it at three days?' corrected Gogarty. 'For one day.' As a matter of fact, Jim has a reputation altogether out of keeping with his merits. Within the last two months he has been only once drunk, and showed signs of drink not more than three times. Nor is he a person that is easily made drunk, for though he is slight, he is healthy and clear-headed and not at all excitable. Colum said, 'He is going in for the Feis Ceoil [1] now. He came over to me to borrow ten shillings to enter. I hadn't it so he was

1. The Festival of Music, which was to be held on 16 May. Joyce entered the competition and won the bronze medal. He failed to gain the first prize only because he could not read music at sight.

looking all over town for it. At last,' said Colum, 'we managed to enter him.' Colum had really nothing to do with Jim's entrance. Jim got the money by selling the ticket of some of his own books. The truth is, Gogarty—and his mother believes him—hopes to win a literary reputation in Ireland. He is jealous of Jim and wishes to put himself before him by every means he can. The carelessness of reputation is the particular lie he has chosen to deceive himself with. Both Gogarty and his mother are mistaken, however, for Gogarty has nothing in him and precious little character, and is already becoming heavy, while Jim has more literary talent than anyone in Ireland except Yeats—even Yeats he surpasses in mastery of prose, and he has what Yeats lacks, a keen critical intellect. If Jim never wrote a line he would be greater than these people by reason of the style of his life and his character. Gogarty told Jim this incident but Jim has such a low opinion of these Young Irelanders it is really beyond their power to hurt him. If Jim thought there would be a chance of his getting it he would ask Colum for money tomorrow with no very definite idea of paying it back. Jim says he should be supported at the expense of the State because he is capable of enjoying life. Yet Gogarty has friendship for Jim.

This house should be known as the 'House of the Bare Table'.

Shallow Gogarty—'a whirl-wind of pot-bellied absurdities with a fund of vitality that it does one good to see'.[2]

I think Jim's sense of honour is altogether humoursome.

Gogarty tells Jim's affairs to everyone he knows. He told

2. MS note: 'No, he's very tiresome after the first ten minutes.'

a whore called Nellie that Jim was going in for the Feis, and that he had to feed himself on what he got from books he sold, there was so little at home. At this Nellie was astonished, and having taken a liking for Jim,[3] said that if he came in to her she'd give him whatever she had, 'but you couldn't suggest that to him, he's too fuckin' proud.' She has a great admiration for Jim's voice and says that he has the fuckin'est best voice she ever heard.' 'I could sit listening to you all night Kiddie.' Having, I suppose, a taste for chamber-music, she offered to accompany Jim on the 'po' on one occasion when he was about to sing. Jim, who has never lain with this whore by the bye, likes her. In moments of excitement she exclaims, 'God's truth I hate you. Christ, God's truth I do hate you.'

[20 *April 1904*]

Jim is living in lodgings in Shelbourne Rd[1] on money Gogarty lent him, and Byrne and Russell.

A certain sea-captain Cunniam keeps a public-house in Kingstown.[2] He is a drunken vulgarian, with an American accent, a friend of Pappie's. In one of the upper windows of the house a large statue of the Blessed Virgin is conspicuous. I call him Captain Cunniam of the Shrine in Kingtown.

When there is money in this house it is impossible to do

3. Nellie lives on, in *A Portrait of the Artist* and in the 'Scylla and Charybdis' episode of *Ulysses*.
1. With a family named McKernan.
2. Thomas Cuniam, of Upper George St.

anything because of Pappie's drunkenness and quarrelling. When there is no money it is impossible to do anything because of the hunger and cold and want of light.

Pappie seems to think it preposterous that we should expect him to support us until we are settled.

It is not edifying to hear Pappie even when sober taunt his children with their deformities. 'Ye dirty pissabed, ye bloody-looking crooked-eyed son of a bitch. Ye ugly bloody corner-boy, you've a mouth like a bloody nigger.' 'Ye black-looking mulatto. You were black the day you were born, ye bitch. Ye bloody, gummy toothless bitch. I'll get ye a set of teeth, won't I, etc.'

I suggested to Jim to call his verses 'Chamber Music'. The incident with the whore is surely an omen.

My spiritual life has been very slight, but constant.

[*20 April 1904*]

I am not afraid of Hedda Gabler but I was when I knew her first. I think I like her perhaps better than Jim, though I don't understand her as well. Jim is Eilert Lövberg, and the oracular authority on Hedda in Britain. She is the highest type of woman I know.

This is not a diary or a journal written to be kept and possibly—we are vain in secret—published. Though it is written carefully, even painfully, I appreciate that it is badly written because I do not know myself. These are notes made for my private help.

[*23 April 1904*]

I am reading Marie Bashkirtseff's Journal. What a hotch-potch! A journal such as that is not worth publishing. I think much more than she does in a day—not unfrequently original matter of importance—and would not consider it worth while putting it in these notes, much less printing it. She does not know herself and therefore tells lies. I lay down the book many times and I try to know her but it is too troublesome when I do not know myself. I fancy if she had become a singer she would have had the applause and life she wanted and her other gifts would have adorned her monument. She was evidently no artist and though singularly clever she has not the deep, strong, logical prob-ing of the sane mind which is intellect. She has written her journal because she has not the continence to keep silent until she knows herself. She must have been a fine contralto —for contralto I presume from her temperament it was. (It was a mezzo-contralto she says later.)

[*16 August 1904*] [1]

I doubt if I will ever sing well. I have not much voice and I have a delicate throat. It would want to be saved and well trained and made the most of—and my temper is too

1. The date, though out of sequence, is clear in the margin of the manuscript.

violent for that. Today I got up at about one—there is no reason why I should get up earlier. I found my boots gone. I rang for them and was told Poppie had taken out the laces to give them to Pappie early in the morning. As both Pappie and Poppie were out and there were no means of getting laces, I thought I would have to walk about in my socks all day, unable to go out. I shouted and cursed, thumped the deck and called for the boots to be brought up anyhow, and bawled out foolishly that laces must be got somewhere. Eileen and Florrie[2] were frightened, and Florrie brought me up my boots gingerly. My throat felt burning, sore and frayed, and that annoyed me. It is really unfair when I need so little and keep my things so long, that that little should not be left with me. Pappie has my coat, gloves, and laces, Jim my rain cloak and this morning wanted my hat, and these are clothes that are much older than their own. It was all over in a few minutes and I was sorry for my unphilosophic incontinence. I shall tell this to Aunt J.[3] when Katsy is there and obtain absolution—we need confession. Shall I though? No. This is silly.

Jim has an irritating trick of disappointing one.

[3 April 1904]

In a room I am self-hypnotised. I see only the chair I am going towards or the person I am talking to in a chaotic

2. Florence, age 10 at this date, was the youngest child except for 'Baby'.

3. Josephine Murray was the wife of William Murray, brother of Mrs. Joyce.

fashion. But let us once go outside in the open air and I take the upper hand.

Paidraig MacCormack Columb [1]—the messenger-boy genius.

I am not able [to decide] for myself. My mind suggests too many by-considerations when I attempt to decide rationally on any matter.

I feel like a blind man, that is, my outlook on life is not clear. It is my endeavour to live in a clearer world.

I dislike lies, yet I tell them and often without reason. They encompass me. Nevertheless it would often be offensive to speak the truth, and also often too intimate a compliment.

Why should I respect my father, and why, when Jim tells me how he stood up and left when Uncle Willie confessed to him that he hated Pappie, should his pride seem to me the working of a natural and old-fashioned nobility in Jim's perverse and modern character—and a sign of its aristocracy? I envied him that impulse for I am envious. And yet Jim called Pappie 'that little whore up in Cabra' before Elwood [2] for selling the piano on him. Pappie's mind too works towards Jim's with the same backward motion. I know Jim acted purely on impulse. Is it sometimes noble to act on prejudice? Or are they stupid? Or am I? If Jim read this he would probably laugh and throw it at me and say, 'Ye thick-headed bitch.'

I reject scholarship and reading and adventures—such adventures as one meets with by drinking and going the

1. Padraic Colum, poet and dramatist.
2. John Elwood, a medical student, is Temple in *A Portrait of the Artist*.

round of the town, and prefer rather to remain discontented and barren than to satisfy a false appetite.

My soul is fainting with shame at my want of courage, and lies to the world by an erect carriage. I stride in my walk but I am drooping with fatigue in my interior. I have never dared to act as I please, but think in a little way 'what will be thought of it?' 'Will so-and-so be displeased, will so-and-so despise me?' My manner would be complimentary. Women admire most in a man moral courage, and I wish most of all to be worthy to be admired, yet reject the wish itself as unworthy when I have framed it. The devil's advocate in me taunts me with being my own greatest tyrant. But I shall act as little as possible till I know surely, and I will not allow myself to be self-forced into extravagances and imitations of the courageous.

Gogarty is generally regarded as a dangerous companion. He is scarcely this until he is intimate, but he is certainly a most demoralizing person intellectually.

[A leaf is lacking in the manuscript.]

Pappie cannot have been a bad lover when he was newly married for I notice that his manner of fondling Baby, for instance, is very playful and endearing.[3]

· Reflection is my predominate habit. I have the character of a philosopher, without the strong intellectual curiosity and without the intellect. I am slow. I dislike getting up in the morning because rising entails dressing, washing, and coldness, and either interrupts or puts a full stop to my train of thought. Besides, I can think best in bed. I dislike

3. MS note: 'Fudge!'

making beginning, and I dislike reading because books are so badly written and mostly lies. 'Let a man say what he knows, I have guesses enough of my own.'

I would like to be revenged on my country for giving me the character I have.

I have been unhappy all day. I find that the cause is I have been walking on my heels instead of the ball of my foot.[4]

I am tempted seven times a day to play a part, and others encourage me by playing up to me. Let me guard against this and I may become something worth knowing.

I am not more characterless than most people, indeed quite the contrary. But I have been so educated that I can make some pretence to an impersonal judgment of myself. I have blushed all over my body at times at my own ignobility and shrunk from confessing utmost stupidity. Since sixteen or seventeen I have practically done nothing except unlearn the lies I was taught, and I will probably not be myself until I am close on thirty. 'Know thyself'—but if when I know myself, I should discover I know a self not worth knowing, what then O Oracle? I will prophesy this of myself, however, that I will improve with age like good wine. ✓

Pappie is jealous for his children at least—a good point.

One thing can be said of Jim's friends—Colum, Byrne, Gogarty, Cousins [5] and those, that they are good liars. The rest I doubt.

4. Cf. the conversation between Stephen and Maurice in *Stephen Hero*, ed. John J. Slocum and Herbert Cahoon (New York: New Directions, 1955), p. 100.
5. James Cousins, poet and theosophist.

Jim got fourth at the Feis Ceoil tenor solo competition.[6] He did not try the piece 'at sight'.[7]

Charlie has been in gaol for drunkenness. The fine was paid after four days, and he was released. He is in with Jim's medical friends very much thicker than I ever was— *not with Cosgrave* [8] *or Byrne however*.[9] He was something of a hero after this exploit, and lately has been obviously emulating Jim in drinking and whoring. He has slept three nights running with a whore in Tyrone St. His intimacy with the 'medicals' has given him precisely what he most desired, and has relieved me of society that was always too thirsty and dissipated for my taste. Not that I don't like Elwood, for instance, or that O'Callaghan isn't a good-natured, thick-headed fellow, but when together they become very boisterous and gross.

J. F. Byrne is a man who never thinks until someone begins to speak to him. Then he deliberates behind an impenetrable mask like a Cistercian bishop's face, and one is given to understand great mental activity. Having spoken, he pretends to infallibility. The more subtle the conversation becomes, the more brutally he speaks. He is fond of the words 'bloody' and 'flamin' '. My latest name for him is 'Thomas Square-toes'.[10]

6. By withdrawing from the competition in sight-reading, Joyce was reduced to 'honorable mention', but when one of the principal winners was disqualified Joyce rose a step and received third prize.

7. MS note: 'his voice was alluded to in the report, though no other tenor is mentioned.'

8. Vincent Cosgrave, who shared James's dissipations in their university days and later, is Lynch in *A Portrait of the Artist*.

9. Underscoring and marginal comment '!!' in pencil, perhaps by James.

10. Cf. the description of Cranly at the opening of Chapter 22 of *Stephen Hero*.

Cosgrave and I are much in one another's company of late. We agree on many things and our minds follow much the same train of thought. We are intimate, but there is not the faintest trace of friendship. I must guard against it for fear some should spring up. I do not wish to be dependent on anyone's mind except on Katsy's. Friendship with men repels me.

There was never any friendship for Jim in my relations with him for there was never any real trust.

Katsy has at times a sharp look in her face. This look is common in a certain class and I dislike it most in women. Miss Walker,[11] the actress on the Irish National Theatre Company, who is thought here and was thought in London to be so beautiful, has it. Mother had it slightly, and Miss Rathbourne[12] or Mrs. Casey (whichever she is) has no other expression in her face at any time. The sight of Miss Rathbourne irritates me. I would turn down a street to avoid her.

Colum has a gross affectation of manner, an eagerness which is rendered all the more unpleasant by a hard and hoarse voice. His gait is hurried and his eyes without lustre. Altogether he is not a person one would take a fancy to.

MacDonald, a medical student, is I think rarely thirsty, though Cosgrave says he has the thirstiest face he ever saw. It seems to me that his mind needs 'a pint'. I know a provision merchant in Dorset St. whose mind, in the same way, seems to me to need a horse's haunches between the shafts before him, and perhaps Jim's mind needs dissipation.

11. Marie Walker (Maire nic Shiubhlaigh).
12. A Miss Rathbourne lived not far from the Joyces, at St. Alban's Terrace.

There is a third Irish national vice besides drunkenness and masturbation, lying.

When McCormack [13] has been singing piano and he lets out his voice in its full power, it gives you a bang on the ear.

Mrs. Skeffington has a nice little hand and like her sister Mary, a beautiful voice.

Gogarty's hooked nose and pointed chin and rotund form remind me of Punch. He wears a Punch-built waistcoat.

Elwood has a hectic-coloured, blue-tinted face, with an immature, shambling deportment like a young recruit. He has a long head like a gipsy, Jim says. He is reported to be the best chemist in the medical school.

Uncle Willie has made two good phrases. He described the aristocracy waltzing at the castle ball as 'looking at one another like cats'. Describing Georgina Burns singing 'I am Titantia' from 'Mignon', he said that she used to sing the runs with extraordinary flexibility and that she hit the last high 'C' (I think) with a note like the smashing of thin glass.

Palmieri [14] has written to Jim telling him that Denza,[15] the judge at the Feis Ceoil, spoke very highly of Jim's voice and said he would have given him first place but for sight-singing and want of sufficient training. Palmieri is now training Jim's voice for nothing and advises Jim to take to concert singing as a profession.

13. John McCormack, now beginning his rise to fame, had encouraged James to enter the Feis Ceoil.

14. Benedetto Palmieri, leading voice teacher of Dublin, coached James.

15. Luigi Denza, composer of 'Funiculi-Funicula'.

Pride is a good thing for the spinal column.

Aunt Josephine says that Katsy has no secrets from her. If this is true—I doubt it—Katsy has not yet begun to live.

Pappie is a balking little rat. His idea when he has money is that he has power over those whom he should support, and his character is to bully them, make them run after him, and in the end cheat them of their wish. In his face this is featured in his O'Connell snout.

I read, like Katsy learning her lesson, to get words. A good writer uses words justly and I appreciate good writing, but beyond this what is written is often not meant, and very rarely authoritative.

I fail to see the magnificent generosity in standing a drink, much less a drink which nobody wants. It is an idle habit—ballast to fill up empty time and an empty mind. Moreover I understand that the greater number stand drink at somebody else's expense, Jim for instance at the expense of anyone he can 'touch', Pappie all his life at the expense of his wife and children.

The manner in which Uncle Willie tyrannizes his children is to me an intolerable and stupid cowardice. And yet though not bad or low at heart, I think, they are most unruly and ill-reared. They are subdued, even terrorized at home, and regard it as a great pleasure to be allowed to run about the roads. He is [too] stupid to see that they will be obedient only so long as they must. Alice told me that on one occasion Bertie, then an infant of six or seven, begged Uncle William not to beat him and promised to say a 'Hail Mary' for him if he didn't.[16] Such appalling cowardice on

16. James used this incident for the ending of his story 'Counterparts', in *Dubliners*.

both sides nearly made me ill. I laughed as if I had been hurt. His manner of asking his children to do anything is absolutely boorish.

Sometimes when I am walking with another and talking, I begin slowly to fear that I am stupid.

Cyclists are my pet aversion. I have an artist's objection to their bulging thighs and dining-table legs, and an amateur's dislike for their bent-leg diving and style-less swimming.

Life is becoming very difficult. It seems that one must submit to a pettifogging mechanical routine and ugliness in some form, a half-witted, mastering incubus.

My character is permeated by suspicion from constantly listening to Pappie reviling people behind their backs and throwing his hospitality to them in their faces.

Jim considers the music-hall, not Poetry, a criticism on life.

I prefer idling alone, therefore I hate 'knocking about town'.

To any priests who question me about Jim, I shall say he is studying explosive chemistry preparatory to inventing a new torpedo, and a little later that he is writing a novel.[17]

'The thing about Byrne,' according to Jim, is that he is so daringly commonplace. He can speak like a pint.[18]

Both Jim and Pappie seem to be a little proud of having spendthrift blood in them. This is a little ridiculous in Jim at present, as he has nothing to spend.

Jim rarely or never acts on principle, yet some fixed

17. MS note: 'Rot!'
18. Compare James's sketch of Cranly in the opening of Chapter 22 of *Stephen Hero*.

ideas influence his life. I think one of these is an objection to constraint—even self-constraint, never to force any growth in his soul even though he consider it good.

The names of Uncle Willie or Uncle John do not become my tongue or pen.

Women like the cruel look in men because they feel that the spirit which may be cruel to them will also be cruel for them in times of danger, and moreover that the tigers of wrath are wiser than the horses of instruction.

My conduct is, I think, as nearly negative as is practical. I refuse to do anything of definite importance in my life until I have made a rational interpretation of life a basis for living. I appreciate the fact that if I did anything of consequence and with larger experience highly disapproved of it, the reaction would be a satisfying spiritual experience, but I refuse the falsity and artificiality of such a course. Therefore I have not whored, for instance.

Few things are so puzzling as the way in which we submit to dogmatic lies, unless, perhaps, it be the way in which we fail to grasp the obvious.

I have a habit of listening to my thoughts, which somewhat destroys their ingenuousness.

One phrase Georgie used to say of Charlie with great conviction—'Oh the stupid ass!'

I called McCormack's voice 'a white voice'—it is a male contralto.

My constant endeavour is to be articulate to myself.

I call 7 S. Peter's Terrace, Cabra,[19] 'Bleak House'.

19. Where the Joyce family had lived since the autumn of 1902.

About a week ago I went out for a walk with Aunt Josephine and Katsy. Katsy was very difficult, pulling away from me, pretending I was hurting her, and seeming to cry —once or twice, I thought, really on the verge of tears— and was even a little rude without meaning it. I was disappointed and dissatisfied—dissatisfied with myself chiefly for being unable to make the walk interesting without these tricks. I vented my irritation by being ill-mannered. I remained silent. In a few minutes Aunt Josephine asked me in her coaxing manner what was the matter. I said, 'Oh! nothing at all!' innocently, and remained silent. 'Ah! he wants to be petted,' said Katsy as if talking to a baby. This being nearly true—though not by Aunt J.—did not help me out of my ill humour. Aunt Josephine said something to Katsy evidently blaming her. I heard, 'Oh! let him! He'll get out of it,' but as yet she was only half in earnest. Here was additional cause. At Annesley Bridge coming home I spoke for the first time to her and asked her if I was so rough that she began to cry every time I laid hands on her. She said, 'Oh! I didn't cry—did I, Mother?' I said good night to them. Katsy was I believe very much offended and said I was too huffy, that Aunt Josephine wasn't to mind me, and that she would not go for a walk again in the evenings. I met her next day while waiting for Jim. She answered when I spoke to her but managed to be entirely [in]different to me. I had an inclination to stand on my dignity, while I admired the right instinct which led her to take me up so quickly. This little girl of fourteen is quite secure in her manner and very much cleverer than me. I recognised that pig-headed obstinacy was not an heroic virtue. When I was leaving Cabra it seemed very easy to admit I was wrong, but it became more difficult with every step. I was to meet Jim there.[1] He was not there when I called, and Katsy was not in. She came in later. She shook hands but did not speak to me directly, and when I tried to look intimately at her, the slight tendency to a turn was noticeable in her eyes and she looked down quietly. She went down to some kittens in the kitchen. I followed her. I went up to her where she was kneeling at the press, and asked her what was the matter. She said nothing was the matter. I was silent and kept playing with her hair. I felt it very hard to say what I should say. I asked, 'Do you think I have been too huffy with you?' 'That is a matter for yourself.' I was silent again. 'Perhaps I have been too huffy, Katsy.' 'You should try and correct it in your character,' said Katsy, playing with a kitten. This was more than I expected but I did not stop. I spoke to her for a long time, asked had I not any reason, said I would not let a little thing like that stand—. I partly succeeded, with difficulty, in keeping my eyes dry and my voice clear. She spoke more friendly after a while, defending herself, and would have put her own 'huff' down to annoyance on Aunt Josephine's account. I said I was sorry, and later when I said I wanted to see her that evening and she hesitated, I said, 'You don't think I would be "huffy" (as you put it) with you again?' This was the nearest I

1. I.e., at Katsy's. James was not now living with the Joyce family.

could go. I was sorry I did not directly do what I wanted. I felt really relieved and happy, much the same as I used to feel after confession. The next day was her birthday and I made her a small present. It is a humiliating thing to be poor. I would have liked to have made her a valuable one. There is something in Katsy which challenges me. I am deeply dissatisfied with myself, however, for one thing—that I made a clever and I think lying epigram about it. 'It is largely a matter of chance or circumstance whom men make the instruments of their passion.' I am glad now I admitted I was wrong. This submission on the emotional plane seems to have a correspondent on the physical plane in a certain sexual aberration which once obsessed me.[2]

I am of that disposition which would keep a trust for the sake of the keeping, not for the sake of the person trusting.

[23 July 1904]

'There's Katsy!' I saw her tonight from the Annesley Bridge. She ran quickly across the road in the dark and back again. I started at the sight of her. I had been sullen all night. She could not know I was there and saw her. Where did she go? Into Elmore's, run out on her last message before going to bed? No, into my heart and scuttled round it and out again, the little mouse.

I am trying to be wise, and when I cannot be so, trying to pretend that I am.

2. MS note: 'This incident now seems to me sentimental, ridiculous, and to have been put on paper before it was understood.'

I have a habit of making up my mind one way and from weakness of will, want of courage, or stupidity, acting another.

I am delighted with what I have discovered. Katsy did not tell Aunt J. how I apologised or that I did. This loyalty is high flattery. I did not ask her not to, and she is a talkative little girl who has no secrets from her Mother. Moreover they talk a lot about us at Murrays and this incident is sure to have been well analysed.

Jim treats me in a very cavalier fashion.

Aunt Josephine has been very 'mopish' in her manner towards me lately, as if she meant to let me see how indifferent she is as to how her manner affects me.

I have spent the month (July) suffering from people's manners.

Virginian stock has a familiar name, 'Night-stock'. I think this would be a fine fragrant name for whores.

Why should lowness of character be any more blameworthy than lowness of stature? Are we responsible for one and not for the other? Why should not greatness, self-constrained in a little mind, be as ridiculous as an assumption of stature in the gait of a little man?

I admire maturity.

[23 July 1904]

Charlie is in hospital—in the Whitworth Hospital—with incipient tuberculosis of the pleura of the lung. It is self-induced. I do not like to have to go and see him, yet I pity him. I did not appreciate a fine or great character in him healthy. He did not interest me in any one particular way. Why should he now that he is in danger of a life-destroying disease? He remains Charlie. When I think of his chances in life, not merely material prospects, but chances of overthrowing the kingdom of boredom, of winning happiness—a quickening interest in life and the interest, self-unrebuking, of others that attends it—of loving and winning love upon the peaks of promise, I see that they are small, and I cannot regard his possible death as a calamity. But I know how pitiful it would be, for I know with what tenacious blindness we hug our little curs of lives. Perhaps his vanity—a life-lie—might let him live. It is a poor card.

How can I say that I like Poppie when I see that her life is without purpose and without interest. She moves me only to compare her hopeless life to mine. What is the virus of her disease? A forced virginity? Yet I know the unselfish, patient goodness of her character. Is she not wishing really that what substitutes a purpose in her life may be taken away, if she wishes that a steady income may sweep away our difficulties? I have lived as a sucker on the resources of the family and she has suffered thereby, but I am looking for the life that fits me. Why should I limp about in a life too small for me, like a man wearing tight boots?

Somebody said that Jim was very determined. Jim denied saying that like a wise man he was determined by circumstances.

My mind is old.

[*1 August 1904*]

May was let out from Mountjoy St. Convent for today
—Monday, August the first. I think she has become a little
stupider, I'm sure she has become fatter. But I was bored all
day, bored because I had not Katsy, or was not with her. I
found out the reason early in the day. I was bitterly disappointed on the 19th July because I could not go to a
Regatta with Katsy. Katsy was dressed in a light summer
dress. It was a bright day and I like Regattas in the sun,
but above all I like Katsy. I was bitterly disappointed and
the bitterness is in me still.[1]

[*31 July 1904*]

Last night, Sunday night, I was more boisterous than
usual and then became silent. I was put out because [of]
Poppie and Eileen being there. Katsy went all night with
Eileen. They ran past quickly on the path and Katsy
turned her face to me laughing. I felt as if she was tramp-
ling over my liking for her like a charge of cavalry. Alice [1]
said something had annoyed me, and would not believe me
though I told her, 'No,' I was not annoyed.

Mr. Matthew Kane—whom I nick-named the 'Green St.
Shakespeare'—has been drowned in Dublin Bay.[2] I am

---

1 For an expanded rendering of this incident, see pp. 165–167.
1. Katsy's sister.
2. The drowning is mentioned in the 'Ithaca' episode of *Ulysses*.

sorry because this throws Pappie more on me. Pappie depends much on his friends to pass his hours now that his life is lived.

Chopin is a favourite musician of mine; he is, perhaps, the genius of Poland. This is only a guess, however, for I know very little of the Polish people. To me his music expresses a deep, melodious melancholy, or with formal but most supple grace, a cold brilliant revelry; and these, I gather, are the features of the character of an aristocracy, to whom, because of several conditions of life, a naturally despondent temper, and a dark, proud hatred of the power that has overcome them, dancing nightly with haughty and elaborate pleasure is life.

When Jim is away I am not so much lonely as alone.

Jim says that his ambition in life is to burn with a hard and gem-like ecstasy. Mine is then—it would be said—to burn with a hard and Jem-like ecstasy.[3]

The people I hate most are those in whom I see a caricature of myself.

Others who act foolishly or in a low manner fall beneath themselves; I fall back.

I feel, at times, like one who is sick but doesn't know it.

Strangely enough in one whom science irritates and wearies, the subject which most interests me is semi-scientific—energy.

I am tormented by a longing to please and to be liked. I am painfully sensitive and little things sting me like a whip. O Anger, leave me a little peace!

I called Katsy once 'my sly saint'. She looked at me mockingly and said, ' "Your sly saint"! I like that! What

3. MS note: 'After Pater.'

dog died, may I ask, and left you anything?' The phrase is not coarse in her mouth, it is a phrase in their house. Aunt J., who was there, laughed; I laughed and went on talking again. I was checked and hurt but I did [not] let it be seen. It would be ridiculous to inflict my sensitiveness on others. I did not call her 'my sly saint' again, because I did not want to have the incident repeated.

My mind is discontented because I do not know whether I love Katsy. My judgments when I dislike or disapprove seem to me sincerer and truer than my judgments when I like or approve.

Byrne is not near as clever nor half as sane as Cosgrave, but I think there is more in him, that his mind is of a higher type. He wears endless discontent like a hair-shirt, and is deeply dissatisfied with himself.

I think all my confessions when in the Church must have been bad, as in none of them was I ever revealed to myself.

I am trying to be spiritually free.

Many people have suffered as much as Jesus to gain that freedom of spirit the right to which Katsy is willing to resign in becoming a nun.

I like Katsy because I think when she is a woman she will live.[4]

I admire in Pappie, at times, an unspoken, absolutely unangered contempt for his interlocutor. It witnesses a complete superiority and is quite without pity.

The banjo has a comic, nasal voice.

I can imagine an original style of criticism by pointing the stops on which the organist is playing. In a novel, for

4. MS note: 'That is, I like her for the possibilities which I think are in her.'

instance, such a phrase as, 'He was a man slightly over the average height.' Or in Henry James' *Portrait of a Lady*, such a sentence as, 'Under certain circumstances there are few hours in life more agreeable than the hour dedicated to the ceremony known as afternoon tea.'

I have a number of wooden ideals lying rejected in the lumber-room of my brain.

Is thought the motion of grey matter in the head, or is it dependent on but distinct from that motion, just as life is dependent on the action of the heart but is yet not a heart-beat nor a succession of them?

Gogarty acts on ill-formed, hastily conceived theories of conduct and thereby causes not a little inconvenience to his friends. As he was once a champion cyclist, I called him 'Last-lap Gogarty'. Need I say that his theories never work out against himself.

Jim, who once considered that J. F. Byrne had signs of genius in him, now thinks he has been very much mistaken. He calls him 'His Intensity' and 'the sea-green incorruptible', and says he is the only man to play the comedy with him (Jim).

The possession of money changes Jim very much for the worse. His mind seems to go on fire for dissipation, and he becomes hasty, overbearing, and impolite. His dissipation has disimproved him greatly. His mind has become a little vulgarised and even brutalised and insincere.

Pappie is trying to escape from the boredom of his life. This is the cause of his tears really if he only knew it.

The catechism remarks that St. Paul says of apostates, that 'it is impossible for them to be renewed again to penance', that is, their conversion is extremely difficult. It says, 'Why is the conversion of apostates so very difficult?' Answer: 'The conversion of apostates is very difficult because by their apostacy they sin against the Holy Ghost, crucify again the Son of God, and make a mockery of him.' This wholesale begging of [the] question and neat shutting to of a false door, so that others may be deceived as to how the free ones escaped, are an admirable mixture of simplicity and roguery and very typical of the Catholic Church.

How am I to live? Not gain an income, not educate myself, become clever—but how to eradicate boredom? I reflect my thoughts on paper so that I may know my state, but I must operate on myself. I must do something. I must know myself and the life that fits me, and act rightly out of my true character. But I fear I shall ultimately remain what I was born.

A master in Belvedere College said I was talking heresy once when I declared that I did not think any act was ever inspired by a simple motive. He said I should believe that Christ died for the pure love of us. I remained silent.

Pappie has been drunk for the last three days. He has been shouting about getting Jim's arse kicked. Always the one word. 'O yes! Kick him, by God! Break his arse with a kick, break his bloody arse with three kicks! O yes! Just three kicks!' And so on through tortuous obscenity. I am sick of it, sick of it. I have a disposition like a woman, and I am sick of this brutal insistence on indignity. I writhe under it. I try to regard [it] as drunken, drivelling lip-excrement, but it is too strong for me. Ugh! It is a word that is scarcely ever out of Jim's mouth. He has been re-marked for it and *playfully* accused of being a bugger be-cause of the way he pronounces it.

Oh how it shamed me! What a sinking of the heart it gave me to hurry down at nine in the morning amongst a number of other clerks to my office! To my office! Ugh! [5]

I love listening to barrel-organs, not to piano organs. They have such quaint old airs and they grind them so slowly. They remind me of the south of France, of oranges, of Spain, that I want to live in.

[*13 August 1904*]

My life has been modelled on Jim's example, yet when I am accused, by my unprepossessing Uncle John or by Gogarty, of imitating Jim, I can truthfully deny the charge. It was not mere aping as they imply, I trust I am too clever and my mind too old for that. It was more an appreciation in Jim of what I myself really admire and wish for most. But it is terrible to have a cleverer elder brother, I get small credit for originality. I follow Jim in nearly all matters of opinion, but not all. Jim, I think, has even taken a few opinions from me. In some things, however, I have never followed him. In drinking, for instance, in whoring, in speaking broadly, in being frank without reserve with others, in attempting to write verse or prose or fiction, in manner, in ambitions, and not always in friendships. *I think I may safely say I do not like Jim.*[1] I perceive that he regards

5. This paragraph is deleted in the MS.
1. MS note: 'See later' (i.e., pp. 75 and 143).

50

me as quite commonplace and uninteresting—he makes no attempt at disguise—and though I follow him fully in this matter of opinion, I cannot be expected to like it. It is a matter beyond the power of either of us to help. He treats me badly, too, in his manner, and I resent it. I shall try to remember the articles of the creed which I have gathered from Jim's life—the individual life that has influenced me most. He has ceased to believe in Catholicism for many years. It is of little use to say that a man rejects Catholicism because he wishes to lead the life of a libertine. This is not the last word that can be said. Libertinism will, doubt it not, be clever in its own defence. To me one is as likely to be near the truth as the other. There is need of a more subtle criticism, a more scientific understanding, a more satisfactory conviction than is given by such a wholesale begging of the question. Begging questions is a habit with Catholicism. Jim wants to live. Life is his creed. He boasts of his power to live, and says, in his pseudo-medical phraseology, that it comes from his highly specialized central nervous system. He talks much of the syphilitic contagion in Europe, is at present writing a series of studies in it in Dublin, tracing practically everything to it. The drift of his talk seems to be that the contagion is congenital and incurable and responsible for all manias, and being so, that it is useless to try to avoid it. He even seems to invite you to delight in the manias and to humour each to the top of its bent. In this I do not follow him except to accept his theory of the contagion, which he adduces on medical authority. Even this I do slowly, for I have the idea that the influence of heredity is somewhat overstated. Yet I am rapidly becoming a valetudinarian on the point. I see symptoms in every turn I take. It seems to me that *my* central nervous system is wretched, and I take every precaution my half-knowledge suggests to revive it. In his love of life I find something experimental, something aesthetical. He is an artist first. He has too much talent to be anything else. If he was not an artist first, his talent would trouble him constantly like semen. For the things that go to make up life, glory, politics, women (I exclude whores), family wealth, he has no care. He seems to be deceiving himself on this point and it gives his manner a certain untrustworthiness and unpleasantness. His nature is naturally antagonistic to morality. Morality bores and irritates him. He tries to live on a principle of impulse. The justification of his conduct is the genuineness of the impulse. The Principle is itself an impulse, not a conviction. He is a polytheist. What pleases him for the moment is his god for the moment. He demands an absolute freedom to do as he pleases. He wants the freedom to do wrong whether he uses it or no, and for fear he should be deceiving himself by any back thought he is vindicating his right to ruin himself. He accepts no constraint, not even self-constraint, and regards a forced growth, however admirable in itself, as an impossible satisfaction. This kind of life is naturally highly unsatisfactory and his conduct bristles with contradictions. For instance, he practises exercises for the voice regularly; he works at his novel nearly every day saying that he wants to get his hand into such training that style will be as easy to him as singing. The inconsistency might itself be called an impulse but that he mentions both practices as proofs of the power to do regular work that is still in him. Above all, he has spoken with admiration of Ibsen as a 'self-made man'—

partly of course for the pleasure of using this formula of commonplaceness of so singular a man.[2] I find much to puzzle me and to trouble me in the antinomy between the Exercise Monopoly and idea of systematically improving myself—by becoming a scientific humanist (laws which I loathe but which seem my only hope)—and the Principle of Simple Impulse, which pleases me greatly and which seems to me to be the right First Principle in regarding life because the most natural. ('Natural' suggests a private judgment of my own on life. I think the art of life should imitate nature.) I live in a state of intimate and constant dissatisfaction because this Principle seems logically unpracticable. In the love of Philosophy I have not followed Jim, I forestalled him. I even tried, between sixteen and seventeen, to write a Philosophy (I suppose it would have been called a Metaphysic), but having written about nine pages of it and finding that my interpretation of life was a little too simple to be interesting, I burnt the leaves. To say that any course of action is irrational is enough to condemn it in my eyes, but unfortunately not enough to make me dislike it. Indeed, saying that it is rational seems perilously like saying it is commonplace. Mediocrity is a poor relative of mine that 'I can't abear'. The golden mean is as abhorrent to me as to Jim. It will be obvious that whatever method there is in Jim's life is highly unscientific, yet in theory he approves only of the scientific method. About science he knows 'damn all',[3] and if he has the same blood

2. MS note: 'He reconciles this impulsiveness with an exalted opinion of Philosophy. He upholds Aristotle against his friends, and boasts himself an Aristotelian.'

3. I.e., nothing.

in him that I have he should dislike it. I call it a lack of vigilant reticence in him that he is ever-ready to admit the legitimacy of the scientist's raids outside his frontiers. The word 'scientific' is always a word of praise in his mouth. I, too, admire the scientific method, but I see that it existed and was practised long before science became so churlish as it is now. On one point allied to this I differ with him altogether. He wishes to take every advantage of scientific inventions, while I have an unconquerable prejudice against artifice—outside special appliances and instruments. Bicycles, motor-cars, motor-trams and all that, seem to me wanton necessities, the pampering of an artificial want. As for such sensual aids as Herbert Spencer's ear-caps,[4] they seem to me most revoltingly mean and undignified. And to Jim, too, I have forced him to admit. Even from an inventor's point of view, I am sure they are wretched, for there is a great disproportion between the end effected and the means taken.

Jim boasts—for he often boasts now—of being modern. He calls himself a socialist but attaches himself to no school of socialism. He marks the uprooting of feudal principles. Besides this, and that subtle egoism which he calls the modern mind, he proclaims all kinds of anti-Christian ideals —selfishness, licentiousness, pitilessness. What he calls the domestic virtues are words of contempt in his mouth. He does not recognise such a thing as gratitude. He says it reminds him of a fellow lending you an overcoat on a wet night and asking for a receipt. (Gratitude is, after all, such an uncomfortable sentiment—thanks with a grudge at the

4. Herbert Spencer, in chronic ill health, suffered from inability to sleep.

back of it.) As he lives on borrowing and favours, and as people never fail to treat him in their manners as a genius while he treats them as fools, he has availed himself of plenty of opportunity of showing ingratitude. It is, of course, impossible for him to carry out his ideas consistently, but he does the best he can.[5] He says that no man has so much hope for the future as he has, but as he is the worst liar I know, and as he is rapidly acquiring a drunkard's mind, he seems so far as his own possible progeny is concerned to have precious little care for it. Catholicism he has appreciated, rejected and opposed, and liked again when it had lost its power over him; and towards Pappie, who, too, represents feudalism to him, his mind works perversely. But his sense of filial honour, as of all honour, is quite humoursome. What is more to the point is this: why should Jim proclaim his own selfishness, and be angry at the selfishness of others toward him? I am so far with Jim in all this that his idea of modernity is probably a corollary of my theory of genius being a new biological species. I have many theories. And, moreover, I find something stodgy and intrinsically unsatisfying in morality.

Many things he has expressed I remember, for they seemed to me to be just while they seemed to suit me. His contempt, for instance, for enthusing, for strenuousness, for flirting and sentimentality, which he says he leaves to clerks. (He walks out at night with Miss Barnacle, and kisses her, while she calls him 'my love', though he is not a clerk.) He has said that what women admire most in

5. MS note: 'In fact he is trying to commit the sin against the Holy Ghost for the purpose of getting outside the utmost rim of Catholicism.'

men is moral courage, and that people are unhappy because they cannot express themselves, and these things I recollect and at times consider, and though they seem small, they affect me greatly. This is Jim's religion—his faith is probably a little different—so far as I can draw up its articles. The experiment of his life has, I think, less personal interest now than formerly, though he is still capable of holding judgment on himself with a purity of intention altogether beyond my power. Yet should he discover that his interest was mainly experimental, he would consider it an unpardonable self-deception to try to infuse into it a personal anxiety. He is in great danger of himself. I see the way his conduct prevaricates to an unsatisfied mind. He has not the command of himself he once had. He has been in the power of his friends lately, and has needed to be rescued by Cosgrave's instrumentality from them. A year ago he would have rescued himself. He has always read these notes, for there was always much in them about him, and if I was calling them anything I would call them 'My journal in imitation of Jim', but I think his influence on me is becoming less than it was. *August 1904.*

May is beginning to live. She has been asking Katsy has she changed—changed in manner she meant. Katsy said she didn't see any change in her. May said she thought she had become horrible in her manner—stupid you know. The Murrays think May clever. She is clever.

My diary is not very startlingly frank, for I am not overcommunicative even to myself.

Women admire originality almost as well as moral courage, and I think they like it not less.

I am incongruously envious. I envy Jim, for instance,

what Catholics would call 'the purity of his intentions'. His manner, his appearance, his talents, his reputation I do not envy him. When I do envy him anything—the strength of his emotions, the beauty of his mind at times, his sense of honour, his pride, his spontaneity—I do so impersonally. I do not really envy him but his state of mind.

Miss Barnacle has a very pretty manner, but the expression on her face seems to me a little common. She has magnificent hair.

There is one thing which will save me, though I change ever so much, from becoming absolutely commonplace. I shall always regard life as an activity of the spirit, which is capable of yielding spiritual satisfaction. I shall always regard this spiritual satisfaction as the highest good, and shall never accept life as a disciplinary habit which may be made more or less pleasant.

I have nick-named myself 'Il Penseroso'.

I think Meredith's title *One of Our Conquerors* would apply very well to the priests in Ireland.

One of my chief reasons for keeping these notes is to prevent myself becoming stupid.

Jim has a face like a scientist. Not an old fumbler like Huxley or Tyndall, but like one of those young foreigners —like Finsen or Marconi.

Have you ever hummed all day an air you loathed? Have you ever been unable to rid yourself of it no matter how you tried? Have you ever thought thoughts you loathed and been unable to silence them in you no matter how you loathed yourself for them? We are no more responsible for these thoughts than for our dreams. Yet we do not hold ourselves guiltless.

'There is a man who lives in Cork,
A man of great renown,
Because he has a maxim which
He preaches round the town.
He's been a family doctor ever
Since his very 'teens,
But he made his great discovery when
A student at the Queen's.'

'O Dr. Dooley! O Dr. Dooley!
The nation owes a great big debt to you,
For "It's masturbation
That kills a nation,"
Said Dr. Dooley-ooley-ooley-oo.'[2]

Poppie is the most unselfish person I know. She is obstinate and inclined to answer back a great deal, but she is gentle and takes the affairs of the house very much to heart. She seems to wish, if anyone is to suffer, that she should be the victim. What an extraordinary sense of duty women have!

Jim cares nothing, he says, what others think of him, yet I know his pride must suffer from being subjected to their manner as much as I do.

I am always talking within myself, sometimes struggling

1. The date, far out of sequence, is probably that of his hearing the verse.
2. MS note: 'A nasty fact not cleverly parodied.'

to word thoughts, sometimes, most frequently, remembering music, sometimes repeating mechanically phrases and rhymes which are often without even a shadow of meaning. Often some trifling incident is the genesis of a long rambling adventure of which I am the hero, till I suddenly return on myself and see my foolishness, and feel myself left naked to the ridicule of the normal mind without, and my habitual self-contempt within. Sometimes within myself and not quite spontaneously I take up the phrases of the passers-by as they meet, and curse at them. 'O, how are ye?' 'Very well, thank you, ye drink-sodden, foetid-souled clown!' Or, 'Ah, is this yourself?' 'Who the devil else should it be, ye little clerk! Ye consummate common cad! Ye dapper little bastard!' And at times becoming suddenly silent within, I feel like one who, walking at night noisily along a road singing and whistling to himself, stops suddenly to listen.

Aunt Josephine tells me I underrate myself and that I am not an egoist. The fact that I think so constantly about myself should prove to her that I am. Yet I take myself at Jim's valuation of me, because it is my own, perhaps.

At any crisis of his life, in any times of importance, in times when he has money and notoriety, Jim's life separates from mine. When these have passed after a while, we seem to come together again. *Et je m'en fou, je reste dans mon trou.*

[*6 August 1904*]

A few days ago Jim, as is his custom, read these notes of mine. He read them quickly and threw them down without saying a word. I asked him did he finish them. He said, 'Yes.' 'Did you read them all?' I asked with intention. 'O yes,' said Jim with a short laugh at his own frankness, 'all except the part between yourself and Kathleen.' What he implied seemed to me true, so I said nothing, but I may tell that my secret soul was wounded. When Jim had gone, after some time, I took up the notes and read that part again.[1] It did not bore me.

I number among the happiest moments of my life those moments when, as a child locked into a dark room, I ceased from crying and listened to the strange noises downstairs of talk and the clatter of plates of the rest of the family at dinner late in the evening.

Cosgrave paid me a very high compliment in conversation to Jim in my absence. There was some question as to whether Jim was in love or not. Cosgrave told him he was, and that this love was the first of a hundred and that it would not last. He told him that he was not the man to be the protagonist of such a love as the novelists speak of— one love enduring forever—that if any man he knew was capable of this it was I.

I have been paid many compliments—by Aunt Josephine and by Cosgrave. I have been told that some prefer me to Jim. Before one's face praise comes always a little insincere, but when the words are told me and I respect the person I am grateful as for a gift. Yet I think no more of myself for that, being convinced, however much I may esteem his judgment, that in my case it is at fault. I am not sure but I think a little less highly of him because he has a high opinion of me. This is truth. (The first in whom I was

1. See pp. 40–42.

conscious of this disappointment was Fr. Henry,[2] who was Rector of Belvedere and my master for some years. Dempsey,[3] the English master with whom I was very familiar— told me he had a very high opinion of me. 'High opinion of me in what respect?' 'In every respect,' said Dempsey. I was genuinely surprised that a man of his discernment should make such a mistake, and I began to remember certain incidents which should have undeceived him.) [4] When I despise the person—as in the case of Bergan [5]—I set no value on his good opinion, yet I cannot deny that it pleases me. I see that it is often only a way of saying that he is afraid of Jim—we are, of course, constantly compared in their minds—that it is often insincere, and that it is always a reproach, since what he considers good must to my thinking be undistinguished and vulgar. The opinions of me that I am inclined to trust are those into which people are surprised, for I know that when they set about giving an opinion they cannot really say what is on their minds. Therefore I trust more Jim's exclamations or an incident like this. One night, some years ago at Sheehy's, we were playing a game called the 'School for Scandal'. The game consists in someone going out, and everyone in the room saying something about him. He has to guess who said the different things. It is an amusing game. This time Dick Sheehy was out and Maggie was taking down the re-

2. Fr. William Henry taught Latin and Greek.

3. George Stanislaus Dempsey, a lay teacher, the Mr. Tate of *A Portrait of the Artist*.

4. MS note: 'Generally, too, I come to the conclusion that I am a good hypocrite.'

5. Alfred Bergan, a crony of John Joyce, appears under his own name in *Ulysses*.

marks. When she came to me I said that Dick was elephantine in wit and in person. Maggie wrote it down, looked at me for a second, and then said confidently, 'Oh, he'll never think *you* said that!' I said nothing. The quite Parisian compliment passed unnoticed, but I noticed that she was betraying the opinion of me which was held there when I was thought of. I have at least this character of the observer. I have a memory for compliments and their opposites. I confess I find all this obstinate self-distrust very tiresome.

What use is all this writing to me when, for instance, there is no dinner in the house? I ask myself this question but I do not face the answer. What use are my thoughts to me when they do not make me either distinguished or clever, and do take up that time which I might spend in such a way as to gain a competency and win security? I do not see why I should renounce them and am not sure that I could do so even if I wished. It would seem like the renouncing of ambition. I have had two strange impulses lately. One was to try to make money, the other to give up my struggle to be anything but commonplace. The idea of suicide has never been anything more to me than a philosophic contingency.

I persuaded Jim once to read Turgenieff's *Diary of a Superfluous Man*, for I had an idea about it. I asked him what he thought about it. He said he thought the man very like me. This was my idea too. Can anyone blame me for taking Jim's valuation of me when we agree so well about it independently?

I want to be washed and left out to air—washed inside though. I seem to have toad-blood in me. I have never been either virginal or spontaneous, ingenuous or boyish. The springs of happiness are soiled and sickened in my sick mind.

I have sympathy with Dean Swift. His sullen and saturnine character, consumed with dull rage against his people, has much in it that I fully understand. Yeats says that he made a soul for the gentlemen of this city by hating his neighbour as himself. If the Irish had as deep-rooted and constant a loathing of England as I have of Ireland, there would be no need for agitation.

Yeats, by the bye, says also very wittily that the Irish think in packs.

They are all asking me, 'What is the matter with me?' 'What's wrong with me?' I hardly know.[6] I am in doubt and have some idea of holding an inquiry *in camera*. I do not trust people's minds towards me and I do not like anyone sufficiently well to speak to them what is in my mind. What could I say to them in any case? How dull and uninteresting such a talk would be! I ask myself whether I am not deceiving myself and the other when I show affection, and this doubt leaves my manner uncertain. I do not please myself when I laugh and talk with them. I am oppressed by the want of understanding myself and many other matters. I feel barren and ungenerous, dissipated and stupid, but I am less dissatisfied with myself when I am silent.

I like very much a portrait of a young noble by Sanchez Coello, a Spanish painter of the sixteenth century.

It seems to me that much of the mystical discussion be-

6. MS note: 'When they ask me coaxingly what has annoyed me I am angered, because my silence seems without reason. I tell them "Nothing"—the truth——but they do not believe me and begin to treat me sulkily.'

tween writers—especially moderns—comes from their imperfect expression of their thoughts or their unwillingness to develop them patiently.

Antiquity is a time of which old men, being given but scanty and malleable knowledge about it, amuse themselves like children making theories and building commonwealths. It is an unpardonable credulousness to mistake these for anything but imaginary histories.

Death is a very complete ending, an irrelevant, unanswerable, brutal argument, a decision at last in an unready life. There will be the memory of me when I am gone, for a little while. What good is remembrance to me? I shall not remember. The additions to my life and knowledge were daily getting longer, but death has drawn two neat red lines under them and written down nought as total. But the sinking at the end, the fainting, the ecstatic weakness, the surrender, the cowardly knowledge that nothing more can be expected of you—this indeed is a consummation devoutly to be wished for. What if only we could gain something greater than life by living?

The Irish are morally a cowardly, chaos-loving people, quarrelsome and easily deceived, dissipated in will and intellect, and accustomed to masters, with a profitless knowledge of their own worthlessness, which causes them constantly to try to persuade themselves and others that they are what they are not. The lying, untrustworthy, characterless inhabitants of an unimportant island in the Atlantic.

The Inquisitive, the Mnemonic, and the Rational and Deductive Faculties—a trial division of the human intellect.

In Chopin's waltzes the mood is weary and languorous, but the melody seems to have a separate brilliancy.

I remember the morning I finished the *House of Sin*—a damp, yellow morning. The book [7] satisfied me quite, and left me a personal sadness. I went out into the garden. It was humid there. The black earth of the path was flecked under the trees with shade and light. The disc of the sun was large, brimming over with rich, yellow, melting light falling on the ground in heavy drops. There was little noise, for the carts made no rumbling along the soft road and the voices of children did not carry far.

I remember also a scene of my disappointment. Pappie had asked Uncle Willie up. I was expecting 'an evening'. Aunt Josephine came. Uncle Willie was to follow her if he could, she said. I persuaded Pappie to come with me down to Fairview and bring Uncle Willie up. This although I disliked Uncle Willie, but so that Pappie would have someone to talk to. Alice answered the door at Maria Terrace and told us Uncle Willie had gone out. Pappie had been prophesying this all the way down, but he pretended to believe and left word what he had called for. The truth was, Uncle Willie had some writing to do at home, but besides he was envious of the house, I think, and has disliked Pappie himself secretly since first he knew him I am sure. He had taken offence at some trifle, which I forget and I am sure he does in much the same way as I do with

7. James Joyce had reviewed this novel, by Marcelle Tinayre (1872–1948), in the *Daily Express*, Dublin, 1 October 1903. Its hero, a Jansenist Catholic, resembles in some ways Stephen Dedalus, and its style, changing as the subject changes, points toward a similar technique in *Ulysses*. See Joyce's 'A French Religious Novel,' in *Critical Writings of James Joyce*, ed. Ellsworth Mason and Richard Ellmann (New York: Viking Press, 1959), pp. 121–123.

him. Not so cleverly, I fancy, for people believe me. I am more just to him in my mind however. The incident was one of those little things that irritate. We came home by the North Circular Road. It was a rainy Sunday evening about October, and at Mountjoy the pavement was wet and shining, reflecting the street lamps, and in the sky was one soiled rag of iridescent satin-white in a black storm-cloud. They were at tea when we came in. Pappie went in to the fire in the drawing-room. I went in to tea and told them Uncle Willie was out when we called. They said it was a pity, and after that had been said two or three times there was a momentary silence. Then Aunt Josephine made the obvious remark, 'I don't believe he was.' 'Neither do I,' said I simply, but the laugh I caused did not dispel my disappointment.

I remember other scenes but the emotion they suggest is too slight and too long to tell—a cold night, the lamps of the trams and the street lamps shining very brightly, the stars veiled in an incense of haze—a clear cold night of wind-blown stars, the road and the low walls stretching over the hill very white between green fields—the hushed sound of continuous falling rain, broken by the separate splashes of heavy drops on the sill of the open window.

I have lent the first part of my diary [to] Aunt Josephine. Charlie used to tell her all his boring mind and his worse verse, Jim tells her practically everything, and here am I now. Such conduct, somehow, seems to me very boorish and trying. In her place I should be heartily sick of all three—no, not of Jim, perhaps. Such a surly discontented production as my journal is, is no reading to offer anyone. To be sure I was asked—even pressed—to give it.

I have a strange sentiment towards Jim of late, a sentiment I would not have been capable of feeling a year ago, a sentiment of pity.

I find 'like' almost as difficult to understand as 'love'. Is it that one finds nothing very objectionable to him in a character and something that pleases? I do not understand my own impulses of liking and disliking, of obstinacy or sycophancy, but I try to understand them and I try to purify them with reason.

I have observed a strange phenomenon in myself. I am almost selfconscious in dreams. Here are three examples. I dreamt, for instance, of Katsie, dreamt I was sleeping with her. She seemed to be asleep in my arms while I was awake watching her, but I felt no weight. By a strange freak of my mind, she looked much older—about twenty —her head was fallen back easily and her hair tumbled about her. This was all. But a moment later I returned on myself and noted to tell Aunt J. the dream. I was certainly not awake at the time, but perhaps I was turning toward waking. Again, I have had an involuntary emission at night without any thoughts of lechery. I seemed to be quite conscious that it was involuntary emission and was not deluded into any of the usual orgic dreams, was chiefly, indeed, annoyed at the inconvenience I would feel when I—what? 'Awoke' seems to express the thought that was in my dreaming mind. Yet where would be the difference between such a dream and reality? I could hardly be surer of what had occurred. This perhaps, that I suffered the act— my will at least was asleep—and that I seemed to watch myself all through. This time too, perhaps, I was turning toward waking: I was certainly not awake, for after a blank of some minutes I awoke to find myself wet, to re-member my dream and be surprised thereat (I have dreamt of having involuntary emissions at night without having them). By-the-bye, the Catholic Church has a belief—not generally known—to fit this dirty and somewhat painful trick of nature, a belief in a 'succubus' and an 'incubus'—the word 'incubus' is common enough. These are evil spirits sent by the devil to tempt people in sleep, acting, the incubus (naughty thing!) on women like a man, and the succubus (naughty and I'm sure pretty little thing!) with men like a woman. I suspect [it is] from the incubus that women suffer from involuntary excitements also. I have these discharges chiefly when I have overwrought myself. I propounded the theory to Cosgrave that if a person re-mained perfectly virginal from puberty, neither copulating nor masturbating, he would not have these emissions, as they came, I thought, from habit and from weakness of the tube therefrom—the urethra I think it is called. Cosgrave thought the theory very unsound. But to return to the third example. I have dreamt I was lying in bed here, and have felt myself weak. I remember saying in my mind that I should not be weak, as, though I was taking a good deal of exercise, I had been feeding well for a few days past, and then deciding that my weakness was due to previous short rations. Evidently I sleep very lightly, and apparently my mind is not very much in the habit of deceiving itself. I have never heard anyone mention such selfconsciousness in dreams, unless it is to it Ben Jonson refers when he writes:

—Now let them close their eyes and see
If they can dream of thee

Since morning hates to come in view
And all the morning dreams are true.—[8]

I wish my first dream was true.

I have been happy this evening—quietly, observantly
happy—happy without having done [any] violence to my
mind to attain my happiness. We have had very little food
—no meal at all in fact—and having taken some tea and
dry bread, I washed and went out. Pappie came in sober,
without money, and in ill-humour, just as I was coming
down stairs. I heard him threatening to put me out. I was
inclined to be irritated, as we are this way through his
having spent £2 10s. on himself in the last ten days. I began to curse him but I found it easy after a few seconds to
whistle instead. Why should I trouble myself about this
matter? When there is money he will spend all he can and
reel home drunk in the evening, and when there is not he
will blame everyone but himself. I went out. It had been
raining heavily an hour or so before and the air was sharp.
The foot-path and the façades of the houses were rain-
washed and drying in patches. I took pleasure in observing
the contrasts in colour—a study in grey. The dark grey of
the church, the grey of the side-walk, the terra-cotta
colour of the houses, the freshened green of the clipped
grass in the gardens and of the leaves on the trees at the end
of them, each holding a drop in its centre, the grey—dark
and light—of the dresses of the women passing under them.

8. MS note: 'fudge'.

The road was quiet and busy with trams and many people walking quickly. I took pleasure in the sameness of colour in the streets I went through, marking the slight change. The stone roadway and path now almost dry, the dark brown houses with one startling colour—the bright yellow front of a dairy—the druggists at the corner of the crossing in front, with dark ivy climbing over the house above the shop, suburban but pretty, the fading dusky sun reflected from behind me on the faces of the people. My mind was at rest for a while, my moral *malaise* was gone from me. I had no wish for the things that trouble me and unsettle me, nothing reproached me, and I did not afflict myself to be compared with any other. I was content to remain as I was, alert and quiet; but not altogether content and not altogether quiet, for something I desired most was not here, O intimate ambition. By the time I reached O'Connell Bridge the dusk was beginning to gather. Far down the quays an obscure blue was beginning to fall about the picturesque faded-green dome of the Custom House and to conceal it. The quays were crowded with cars, and coming up out of the traffic was an organ-man between the shafts, a young Italian woman tugging with one arm at the strap, a red handkerchief on her head, her hair blown back from her temples, her broad passionate face thrown upwards with the effort of pulling—tired, thoughtless, and happy. At the top of Grafton Street the sky was a faint blue with a reflection of flesh-tints over the trees in Stephen's Green, holding a bright horned moon, and I fancied the Green an immense park full of shadows and ruined statues and wide lawns of moonlight stretching down to a rippled blue-grey sea bordered by red-stone rocks—a garden to the crescent moon.

Having written this easily and quickly, I had an impulse of disgust for it.

I have often wished to know why it is that, though Pappie supports us indifferently, knows practically nothing about us, shows us a low example, treats those who let him with the highest moral brutality, and holds up before us constantly a low ideal—an ideal of respectability [that] is selfish, snobbish—yet his mind towards us has something I miss in other households. I think it is this, that he wishes and confidently expects that his sons will be different from the sons of other people, even—and this shows a yet higher mind—more distinguished than he, in his own judgment, has been. He has succeeded, I think, but not in a way he understands.[1] Remember, I dislike Pappie very much, he is intolerable to me. I am resolved not to deceive myself on this point, and this resolution may, perhaps, be the beginning of a spiritual life in me. The idea of it seems to satisfy me.

The question as to what I am to do with myself is becoming urgent in me. I do not think it is to be my fate to be a clerk all my life, though I am prepared to do clerking as a means to my ambition. Men travel in the dark and their fate travels in the dark to meet them, and I am prepared to wait until my ambition comes to me. I have a growing confidence—perhaps a foolish confidence—that it will be

1. MS note: 'Moreover, he has always treated us with a kind of equality with an item or two of authority, and did not think it fit to do away with all ordinary politeness in dealing with us. He has tacitly respected our privacy and has not treated us with that contemptuous inconsiderateness, as toward animals, by which fathers try silently to insist on their absolute superiority. He has not been able to be a senseless bully, and we have no reason not to respect him for what he is—our father.'

different from the compromising life I had accustomed my mind to accept as mine. Maybe when it comes I shall find my fate more like myself than I imagine or wish.

[*31 August 1904*]

I have walked a good deal today (about twenty-two miles in all) but I am not sleepy, only pleasantly tired, conscious of increased warmth in my legs and feet. I left Jim at Sandymount [1] at twelve and walked home. I was watching the turns I had come so as not to lose my way, for I hardly know the locality, until I came to Landsdowne Road Station. The lanterns shone brightly at different heights on the gates and the signal posts of the pretty little station in the trees. It was empty. I passed up Landsdowne Road before those big semi-detached houses with their high stone steps back from the road. The people who live in them are well-to-do, I suppose. I liked the night, it was clear and dry. My intimacy with Jim brings me in ways I like. I wrote a note to Pohlman's [2] for him in the G.P.O. on my way through town. I like the City at night, wide O'Connell Street (I have O'Connell blood in me and an O'Connell face. I would prefer I hadn't. The Joyce blood is better) [3] lit with many high opalescent lamps of muffed

1. Where he was now the guest of James and Gretta Cousins, of 35 Strand Rd.
2. Pohlman & Co. of 40 Dawson St. sold pianos and music.
3. Nevertheless Ellen O'Connell brought material advantages to Stanislaus' grandfather James A. Joyce when she married him in 1848. See Ellmann, *James Joyce*, pp. 10–12.

72

glass, deserted but for a few people and a cat nimbling quietly along, the horse walking, without noise but for an occasional shout of laughter from the cabman's coffee booth. Dublin is an old, small, seaport Capital with a tradition. Yes, Dean Swift is the tradition. I go youngly through the late streets hearing a nocturne of Chopin's. Who but Chopin was able to write nocturnes? He lived by night. He is returned to Paris from some revel that has been brilliant, and is standing at this hour in his attic looking out at the open-dormer window. The huge pulse of life is lulled, darkness like a heavy cloud lowers overhead, and straddled roofs shine beneath him from recent rain. A melody is awake and moves with hushed weariness through the black harmonies of night, easily, almost inaudibly, changing to higher keys till light begins to be seen. It was associated in my mind with a memory. Aunt Josephine played it for me in her house on the North Strand when long after midnight I was about to leave to come home to Cabra. Neither dissembled drowsiness nor the changes from warmth into the cold night air could weaken my sense of gratification, for I was well pleased with the night, and I admired Katsy. I thought her nature luxurious and proud— the pride of the flesh. I felt honoured by the admiration of her which had taken me, as if some influence of complex importance had come really and unsought into my life, but I feared and doubted. More than this she was a simple happiness possessing me—*bonum simpliciter*. I had never found in the conversation of those I liked best, half so much pleasure as a word or a look from Katsy, or as even her propinquity could give me. 'Those I liked best.' I seemed to dislike everyone I knew but her, while my unstable admiration and doubting thoughts left me with only forced and crooked words and looks for her. But a simple unhappiness, since I knew that if she was what I thought she was, she would not like me—would even dislike me when she grew to be a woman—for she must be aware of the disingenuousness, the disloyalty, the spiritual coward-ice, the spiritual envy, the calculating dissatisfied egoism, dogged in my dull philosophy, the criminal idleness, the stupid efforts, the immorality of my mind, the want of dis-tinguishing talent, the affectation of dignity and depth of character and passion, the ugliness, in fine, of me, of which I am all too conscious and which has always made it a presentiment of mine that I could never love, or that, if by some miracle I could, the person I would love could not love me. I wished for shame—that plenary indulgence of all the high opinions of others—that it might simplify me, but I was afraid of it because I was afraid of Katsy. I knew, again, that if she was not what I thought her (I saw with a disheartening disappointment in myself that my influence on her was bad, and that the commonness in her character, which had been weakening through Jim, was de-veloping through me) I could not admire her, but I was unwilling to believe that she was not, as to admit it would have been to admit that I had deceived myself with a hope. *Rassure-toi, l'amour viendra; désole-toi, il n'est pas l'ideal de bonheur que tu penses.* Certainly love is very difficult to a modern.[4]

This is like a thing George Moore would write in *Dana*, only it contains a witty remark.

Jim has written a nocturne in prose beginning 'She

4. MS note: 'I am reminded of, "Oh for the days of my youth when I was so miserable".'

comes at night when the City is still,'[5] and a *matutine* in verse beginning 'From dewy dreams my soul arise.'[6]

Jim's style is becoming a little sententious and congested. He locks words of too great weight together constantly and they make the rhythm heavy. I advised him to read Goldsmith or Henry James to gain easy lucidity, but he does nothing now. His lyrics are becoming much of a piece. His last[7] contained a contradiction ('For elegance and antique phrase, Dearest, my lips are all too wise'—the song is both elegant and antique), a mistake ('Mithradates' for 'Mithridates'), the words 'Dearest' and 'Dearer' used with the same accent at the beginning of two lines in the second verse. It has a recapitulary phrase as a close to the second and last verse and as there is not the excuse of length this is something of a cliché.

As Jim has become very weak lately, I thought I might be striding up to him. I met him the other day after a few days and I was glad that my secret thoughts are hidden, for it seemed to me that the difference between us was not a difference of degree but of kind.

My secret thought is the one I do not wish to write, and my present temper the one I cannot write.

I am wrong in saying I loathe Pappie. I have absolutely no liking for him. The injustice of his mind is aggressive and puts me off, the quarrelsomeness of his temper irritates me, and these being pretty constant led me to make a mistake. I am wrong also in saying I dislike Jim.[8] I have no liking for him but I see that his life is interesting.

---

5. Published in his *Epiphanies*, ed. Silverman.
6. Published in *Chamber Music*.
7. 'Though I thy Mithridates were', published in *Chamber Music*.
8. See p. 50.

My opinion of myself is what I write, and is so low probably because I have a very high standard and can judge myself by no other. Perhaps this high standard implies a high temper of mind. I am more inclined to believe that it is the reflection of Jim's nature. It is none the less the only standard I can judge myself by, and is really in the essence of my character.

Jim has spoken frankly contemptuous things of me so often—without any purpose to offend—that it is beyond his power to hurt me now. He and Cosgrave have lately said flattering things of me, but now that he praises it is beyond his power to please. I remember what others think of me very constantly and very accurately.

Katsy had it in her power to give me more pleasure than anyone I knew, and therefore, perhaps, to wound me more. I told Katsy I did not love her. Not in those words, for as she is half a child it would have been ridiculous and out of place. I said I liked her, but not to any great, unusual extent. I told her I wished she was seventeen, not fourteen. At seventeen Katsy ought to have a woman's mind at the present rate.

What is the higher morality? Is it to be able to believe the cleverly untrue things we think about ourselves?

I never saw Jim manage any affair so badly as he has managed his affair with Miss Barnacle.

Jim said once that he was like the Bourbons, 'he never forgot'. I think it would have been more accurate if he and they had said they never forgot injuries.

I resolved not to put myself anymore in the way of Jim's rudenesses. The letter of these resolutions is broken by me, but the spirit of them remains in me.

I am very unstable, pulled about by a dozen contrary impulses. I do nothing of importance that pleases me.

I have at times an elating sense of seeing people for what they are. This is often to see them as less than I thought them, but the view is elating for all that. I even seem better pleased with people for seeing them so.

My mind cannot be so old yet, as I am capable of being thrilled by new ideas. I feel exhilarated sometimes without cause, but I reject this exhilaration just as Luther rejected his false vision on Good Friday. Sometimes in these moments of exhilaration I hear music in my head which I do not remember to have heard before and which excites me not a little. I have thought from this that, perhaps, if I had studied music and could make these sounds articulate I could become a composer. I doubt.

Food is good and warmth is good. This is a good house to learn to appreciate both in. We do weeks on one chance insufficient meal, and a collation in the days I have been stripped of my garments, even of my heavy boots, willingly stripped, to pawn them and feed on them. What kind of adults will we be? I am becoming quite morbid on the point and regard food as energy-stuff. In what manner would we stand sickness?

I have a sure sign that I have no friendship for Cosgrave. Once or twice I thought I had offended him. I was sorry for my own sake to think I had been guilty of rudeness, yet, though I thought it would put an end to intimacy, I was not troubled for that, rather felt a slight sense of freedom to think that someone else I knew had, by no intention of mine even through a vice in me, been brought not to expect any conversation with me different from his conversation with others. I do not like the youthful, light tone that my manner takes with him. I seem to myself like a light, manageable vessel flirting round a four-master. The manner is false for I know my mind is old, and, as it appears to be inevitable, perhaps there is only one remedy, my taciturn remedy, withdrawal.

There is one Mr. James Brady, a police-court solicitor, a brother-in-law of Mr. Bergan, whom I dislike very much. He seems to me a rare type of the common, cute, Irish fool. He is a friend of Pappie's.

There is one, too, Mr. John Clancy,[9] Sub-Sheriff, whom I also dislike very thoroughly. He is regarded with mild awe, chiefly I fancy because of his height. His creatures—and practically all the people he knows are his creatures in the degree of their intimacy—agree that if he had gone to America in his youth he would be President now. I think he should have become a policeman. He has the appearance, the walk, the bossing manner, and the intellect of a policeman. He is elderly and drink-seasoned. Pappie boasts when he is drunk 'O! John Clancy has a wish for me! He'd do a fellow a good turn!' but I think his real idea about him is something like mine. I had an opportunity once of crossing the impostor and it vexes me into the pluck, when I remember it, that I did not take it. I know neither of these gentlemen.

I like Velasquez's portrait 'Æsop' very much. I have a very vivid idea of Æsop, the wise old freed slave, the *fier bourgeois*, and Velasquez's portrait depicts it perfectly. I

9. Long John Clancy appears in *Finnegans Wake* and, as Long John Fanning, in *Ulysses*.

think Æsop was wiser than Solomon, but Solomon was a poet, Æsop was not.

To call Pappie's mind unjust is as distinct a euphemism as to call a drunken fishwoman's abuse unladylike. I dislike him because his mind is opposed, and I am always better pleased with myself when I treat him with dislike.

Jim's style in prose writing many times is almost perfection in its kind, holding in periodic, balanced sentences and passages a great spiritual delicacy. But between these passages, instead of writing quietly and relying on his life-like dialogue, he tortures his sentences in figurative psychology and writes strenuously.

I can neither do nor think anything that pleases me completely; my mind wearies itself among falsities.

I had once portraits of both Meredith and Whitman in the house. I remember comparing the two, as they were both spoken of as nature poets. Meredith had his chin thrust rather pragmatically out, his face wore a refined, eager, witty, penetrating look. Whitman's had a more egoistical air, strange to say, a meditative egoism, an air of day-light mysticism, which is a prejudice against all other activity. He was looking at you quite conscious of your presence but with the eyes of a man who has the rhythm of a song in his head.

The *bourgeoisie* has a settled mind on a few subjects, and has a habit of assuming that all people are as settled and in the same way about them. These people know that God Almighty gave Moses a very difficult decalogue and that Christ pushed matters farther—between you and me—than anyone but himself could go, but after all both gentlemen are very open to common sense. Of other matters they know that every fellow should get a job, and the worth of the job corresponds with the worth of the fellow; that every fellow has a girl and when his screw [10] has been raised he should marry his girl; that every fellow should knock about a bit and see a bit of life, because those that don't marry or that go into monasteries or live out of the world haven't really as sensible a way of looking at things as you or I, but we won't say anything out loud about them, they have peculiar ideas about these things. They may be clever—they go in for a lot of nonsense we wouldn't bother our heads about—but they haven't any go in them, they're not like men at all. But after all, it's only out-and-out blackguards, or wasters cocked up with a little education, or fellows who want to pretend they are different from everyone else, who talk against religion. We blaspheme sometimes when we are worried, out of humour, and hard worked, but we don't mean any real harm. Sometimes fellows' heads get turned from reading too much, but everyone knows that all the great intellects of the world ——. Besides, compared with our Saviour all their little intellects are like rushlights in the sun. When this philosophy of the man-in-the-street is being talked, it is difficult to know what to do. To pick an argument with such opponents would be a waste of wind and time, and to be silent is to seem to acquiesce. One day [11] in the Apothecary Hall a discussion about the Catholic Association was being carried on, and from phrases I perceived that these ideas were latent in their minds. Religious discussions were

10. I.e., salary.
11. MS note: '8th Jan. '04.'

frequent for the Hall was Protestant, and they used to get on my nerves. One fellow—a traveller and a Catholic—was saying that no one that he got orders from cared what religion he was. His listeners all agreed 'Of course not.' 'Do you think, for instance,' said he, 'that if I went in to Dr. Stock [12] to get an order from him he'd care what religion I was? Do you think he'd know what religion I am?' They all agreed 'Not he.' I had been taking no part in the discussion, but I turned round quietly to White—the traveller—and asked ingenuously 'Do you?' They thought it very witty, and White seemed to take it as a compliment. In the laugh, the discussion stopped.

Another of these latent ideas is that a fellow may whore a little and live a little loosely—especially in youth—and no harm, but he should always do so secretly, and, though he may joke about it when he is wild, admit afterwards that it was wrong for him, and when he is older and married he should give it up, and strictly forbid it, and put it down in his sons and daughters above all, remembering that it is his duty not to give bad example, especially by word. The facility with which your wild young fellow adapts his mind to such a contradictory and complex view is really beyond me. I cannot understand such obvious inconsistency and injustice to a younger generation. The day after Mother died a number of people called to sympathise with Pappie. After they had seen Mother in her coffin they came down to the drawing-room and sat there drinking and talking in an undertone. There was Mr. Kane,[13] the late

12. So spelled, but he doubtless means Dr. R. T. Stack, of Merrion Sq.
13. Matthew Kane, who had drowned on 10 July 1904.

chief clerk in the Crown Solicitor's Office, who had to marry his wife, Mr. Devon,[14] who is known to be still a consummate whore, and Uncle John,[15] whose eldest child is a bastard, and who also had to marry the common little person who is his wife. He is now converted, however, except for an occasional 'burst'. He was talking and I was half sitting on, half leaning against, a square piano. The talk changed from subject to subject and at last it came round to some letters that had been written to the papers against a play at the 'Royal'. Uncle John asked me did I ever read any of Zola's and what did I think of him. I was more bored by Uncle John than even by Zola and I answered indifferently and in monosyllables. Then Mr. Kane began to explain—a little awkwardly, I think, because of my presence and with much gesticulation—how he had to read some of Zola's novels—in an official capacity of course—and how they were horrible, horrible. How they could print such stuff—! Uncle John began to relate how—'when he was a young fellow and his taste for reading was omnivorous and his means small' (Uncle John laughed asthmatically) 'he used to go to a second-hand bookseller in High Street. One day he went there to get *The Colleen Bawn*'[16] (Uncle John, whose accent is bad, came down very flatly on 'Bawn'; his taste must have been omnivorous indeed) 'and when he went in the fellow there brought him into the back and showed him some books—. Such ideas to

14. Tom Devin (or Devon), an old friend of John Joyce, is the Jack Power of 'Grace', in *Dubliners* and appears under his own name in *Ulysses*.

15. John Murray, brother of Mrs. Joyce, is the Red Murray of *Ulysses*.

16. Play by Dion Boucicault.

be putting into the heads of young fellows—!' There was a silence to imply the enormity of the books. I was on the point of asking 'Did you buy them?' but I thought it would be very indecorous in the circumstances.[17] I am a damned fool, I always let slip opportunities of getting a neat jolt in the ribs at those I dislike.

I desire the pure, faithful beauty of certitude.

'Judge not and ye shall not be judged.'— This is peddling, winking cowardice. Judge constantly, by all means, without fear and without favour, and as you hope to know yourself, apply your judgments to yourself. I consider Jesus' reply, when taken unprepared by the Jewish accusers of the woman taken in adultery, a witty, sentimental, dangerous equivocation, for it says that if one of them was without sin he might justly stone her. Surely this was not his teaching. The truth is, he did not know what to do, between his wish to save the adultress (I wonder did he know her) and his wish not to cause the laws of Moses to be rejected. But I consider it as cowardly not to condemn vice in others because we ourselves are vicious, as it is jealous not to appraise virtue in others because we wish ourselves to shine.

Admit this uncertainty and imperfection in Jesus and where do you end?

Self-deception on any subject in the working is to choose for some extraneous reason not to harbour doubt about our judgments, and to endeavour to believe that we have judged truly.

I did not appreciate the epithet 'You dog!' until the other day when I was sitting in the window of my room

17. This incident appears in Chapter 22 of *Stephen Hero*.

at the back overlooking into the yard next door. Some birds flew out of a tree in our garden, and immediately an old collie our neighbours keep rushed down their yard and hurled himself against the wire partition enclosing the hens, and kept whipping round in fury with sharp, noisy yappings and panting for breath. After a minute he stopped and came back slowly, growling and stopping every minute with his head up in the air to give a short, angry bark at nothing. An old hag hobbled out of the kitchen with a hen under her arm—there seemed to be some horrible affinity between the old woman and the hen—and the dog began sniffing round her and the hen and wagging his tail out of a sense of duty. Then he heaved up a leg and pissed against a wall and then barked again. I do not like dogs and I like birds less. I think of their lousy feathers and I remember the phrase in the Apocalypse 'every unclean and hateful bird'. I prefer insects and reptiles. Humpy backed spiders remind me of Jews. One of the most astonishing strokes of psychology I know is that of some American (Thoreau, I think) who calls animals nature's dreams. I think to understand their consciousness we must remember our consciousness in dreams. Any novelist who shows a close sympathy with men astonishes, or with women even more. Only a few have tried child psychology, but here is close sympathy with animals.

Jim says my mind secretes bile and that the brilliancy of my mind is mechanical. I did not know that my mind was considered brilliant, and if it is, the standard of brilliancy must have dropped in the last six months. He tells people also that my literary judgments are better than his own. This is said hastily because I criticize his verse and because

I argued about Henry James and Meredith and Tourgeniev with him. Of prose style I know really very little but my taste is, I think, good.

They say you cannot know whether you can do anything till you try, but when I essay to do anything my mind is full of jeers at the effort.

When I read anything witty I have always an impulse—now lessening—to go tell it to Jim.

Jim said one day to Cosgrave and me, 'Isn't my mind very optimistic? Doesn't it recur very consistently to optimism in spite of the trouble and worry I have?' I said 'Yes, to proper optimism.'

Cosgrave told me there was more money in my voice than in Jim's because it was stronger and I would take more trouble with its training if I was having it trained. I do not believe there is very much money in my voice; it is losing its richness, is becoming noisy, and I sing badly.

[*14 September 1904*]

Jim's landlady and her husband have shut up house and gone away on a holiday, and Jim has consequently left Shelbourne Road—for the time being at any rate—since the 31st August. It is now the 14th September. In that time he has stayed first two nights at a Mr. Cousins' [1] on invitation, then a few nights at Murrays, and, being locked out there, one night with a medical student, O'Callaghan. At present he is staying on sufferance with Gogarty in the Tower at Sandycove. Gogarty wants to put Jim out, but he is afraid

1. James H. Cousins and his wife lived at Ballsbridge.

that if Jim made a name someday it would be remembered against him (Gogarty) that though he pretended to be a bohemian friend of Jim's, he put him out. Besides, Gogarty does not wish to forfeit the chance of shining with a reflected light. Jim is scarcely any expense to Gogarty. He costs him, perhaps, a few shillings in the week and a roof, and Gogarty has money. Jim is determined that if Gogarty puts him out it will be done publicly. Cousins and Mrs. Cousins, especially, invited Jim to stay for a fortnight, but Jim found their vegetarian household and sentimental Mrs. Cousins intolerable, and more than this he did not like their manner to him. They made no effort to induce him to stay longer. Jim met Cousins afterwards and Cousins told him that many people had asked them about him and that their household had become quite a centre of interest because he had honored them with two days of his life.

On the 7th, 8th, and 9th of July [I] went in for an exam —the Veterinary Prelim—for a fellow named Gordon. Jim was to have gone in for it but he decided that he was too well known. He asked me to do it instead, and at half-past twelve the night before, I said I would. The exam was very easy and I heard afterwards that I got through. Gordon [2] was to have given Jim 30/–. He gave me 25/–, out of which I shared 14/6 to Jim. I was nearly being caught, for the superintendent knew Gordon's brothers and seeing the name on my paper asked me was I [their] brother. I pretended I was Gordon's cousin, and having taken care to inform myself a little about his people, I was able to answer

2. James Joyce listed a Michael Gordon among friends and acquaintances but did not otherwise identify him (in an alphabetical notebook at Cornell).

the superintendent's family questions fairly intelligently.

Eileen has been staying at Aunt Callanan's [3] for the past month, where they like her very well. They wanted her to stay altogether, but Pappie objected. He said Eileen was not going to become a slavey. Eileen would prefer to stay, but she is to go into Mt. Joy Convent, where May is, on Friday next.

When Jim was explaining what he meant by saying that the brilliancy of my mind was mechanical, he said 'You know, I push myself behind what ever I do.' I certainly reserve myself behind whatever I say or do.

There is no act however bad or low that I cannot sympathise with, and yet there are few acts however noble or good that I do not understand. I find in myself the germ of pure criminal mania, for sometimes when I am walking with a person, whom I like well for the time, and talking quietly, I think with a rush 'if I were to draw out now suddenly and without reason and give this inoffensive person a punch in the teeth——?'

I have a habit when I look at the faces of people of note or of clever or distinguished men in town of examining their heads and features to discover what it is that they have and that I have not that constitutes me their critic. They are nearly always finer looking and bigger, their heads are built on broad lines, they have quick faces with a look of confidence in some well-developed or naturally great power, but to me the expression of their eyes is a little fixed, and can I accuse [them] from this of having unrefined, uncultivated, incomprehensive minds? I think I can;

3. Mrs. Callanan, aunt of the late Mrs. Joyce, lived at 15 Usher's Island, scene of the party in 'The Dead', in *Dubliners*.

their minds are really commonplace; they seem not to see and not to wish very much to know their own purpose; they have none of the 'readiness' which 'is all'; they are tools well fit for the purpose, specialists.

There are no questions which trouble me grievously, yet troubled I am, but not grievously.

Gogarty uses two words well, the Dublinized Jesus, 'Jaysus', and the word 'box'. A 'Jaysus' is a guy. Then there's 'an awful Jaysus', and 'hairy Jaysus', and you can act or 'do moody Jaysus', or 'gloomy Jaysus'. A 'box' is any kind of public establishment, or a hall where any Society holds meetings for some purpose. The rooms of the Hermetic Society are a 'ghost-box', a church a 'God-box', a brothel a 'cunt-box'. He has a good name for priests, too, a strange name in keeping with their ridiculous appearance and manner in the street, the name of certain Chinese priests, the 'Bonzes'.[4]

Nearly all great artists of all nationalities have painted imaginary portraits of Jesus Christ, excusing their ideas by some kind of historical proof, have painted them because they find his character very interesting and because they have perhaps very vivid ideas of him. I, too, have a very definite reading of his character, a little excused in tradition, and I, too, regard him with interest, but quite without religious sentiment—a sentiment never in me. Jesus was neither as simple or as poor as St. Francis, yet how engaging is his simplicity when after his boyish impudence arguing with the doctors in the Temple 'he went down to Nazareth' with his parents 'and was subject to them'. Between this joyous and youthful boy and the strange and sorrow-

4. Misspelled 'Bondses'.

ful criminal, houseless and acquainted with grief, what a difference there is. Jesus was a far more intellectual type than Buddha or Mohammed or St. Francis, though not so beautiful as Buddha nor so masterful as Mohammed nor so charmingly simple as St. Francis d'Assisi. His crises were intellectual not emotional. He seemed to be absolutely without sentiment. During the crisis which wrought the pessimist in him I have no doubt he whored greatly. We know he feasted often with free livers and sinners, and there is no suggestion that he went to them to preach, and we know he was a wine-bibber. He spoke frequently to his disciples' disconcerting [*sic*] with notable whores. Jesus was no eunuch priest.[5] We find something fanatical or foolish always in those who are eternally virginal, something invigourous, unvirile, sentimental. Compare, for instance, a St. Augustine [6] with a St. Aloysius. But Jesus is eminently masculine, unflinchingly wise, knowing man's heart and the world. He praises spiritual ardour and loves it in John and blesses the pure—but the pure of heart. No doubt for some reason (perhaps that he did not advert to it as to a matter of very great importance—there is no carnal temptation in the desert) he acquiesced in his disciples' thinking him a virgin. He even seems to have admired in Peter a blunt simplicity and honesty greater than his own (though in the Garden of Gethsemane he knew its weakness without anger) yet did not overvalue these qualities. He did not attach supreme importance to bodily

5. Compare this passage with the discussion in *Stephen Hero*, ed. Slocum and Cahoon, p. 141.

6. Spelled 'Agustine.' James long misspelled it the same way, though it was his middle name.

purity as his disciples did. To a Catholic this will sound blasphemous, but then Catholics can scarcely believe that he was really enraged in the Temple, yet did he not call them all 'thieves' when they were only traders? [7]

In this, too, he was misunderstood, in his humility; for though it is true 'that humiliated pride falls lower than humbleness', he had very great pride—pride in his ancestry. Indeed, if he was not the son of God he certainly behaved himself as such. He talks of his father [8] with undisguised pride, and of himself—'the poor you have always with you but me you have not always with you.' He doubts if he is the son of God and hates his people—the whited sepulchres —too much for deeds. The clamourous Jewish rabble run to him in their troubles. He is brought in by agitated parents to a fainting girl. He looks at her and says simply, 'The child is not dead but sleepeth.' He is enigmatical and stirs a like temper in others. Yet his few cries of bodily suffering are so simple, so perfect a confession of great weakness—'I thirst'—so classical.

This oriental Jesus is not gentle Jesus, or creeping Jesus, or the *beau jeune homme* of the early Italians, or the preaching moralists [*sic*] of the protestant divines. It might be maintained that the rabblement know nothing of Jesus except that he wept. But the Jesus I have always pictured is the ugly and saturnine Christ of the Good Friday ceremonies, the Jesus of Nazareth who has power over the lightning and who is called upon—not by the Jewish rabble now—to deliver us from a sudden and unprovided death.

7. MS note: 'Mem.—They were Jewish traders.'
8. MS gloss at this point: 'Meredith.'

The Catholic Church is, I believe, nearest to an understanding of Jesus, for in its teaching—not in what it preaches—and in its poet Dante, it is proud, intellectual, and practically contemptuous of morality. If Christianity is to regain respect in Europe it will be with such a Christ, and if it tries to regain its hold by turning democrat, it will lose both its power and its respect.

The portrait Renan has done in his *Vie de Jesus* of '*le charmant docteur*' seems to me not so much like Jesus as like Ernest Renan.

The price of my intimacy with Jim has been clever sayings or little betrayals of myself, and the wittier the turn I can give to these latter the better, but I have lost my taste for these little Judasics, and with it I nearly lost my intimacy with Jim. Jim's intimacy with his friends and theirs with him are also bought at this price—Byrne excepted. Byrne has no unusual abilities or characteristics but he has this, that he can never be induced to betray himself for what he is—whatever that may be.

I am determined that if I break with Katsy it will not be because of any fault in my character, and therefore I have let two or three incidents pass because [it] was not clear to me that I was not at fault. Besides, I like her and it would be not without a certain self-contempt that I would break with her.

Jim was getting into the regular drunkard's habit of paying himself with words.

I have a very instructive habit when I have made a mistake either in acting, in thinking, or in studying, of going back slowly over each step I took, and trying to find out exactly how I was led to make the mistake.

I have moods constantly recurring in which I loathe everything and everyone near me and many I have only seen. Then this house seems to me rotten, useless and decaying, like the hollow tooth I have my tongue in.

I think I dislike anybody who prefers me.

O, I wish the summer was not over, I wish sincerely it was mid-summer and we would have more burning days, the air scintillating with sparks of heat, the sea to swim in, and the fresh breeze from the sea, the rocks and the sand-grass to lie among, and long warm evenings.

Jim used to think Ibsen meant Eilert Lövberg for a genius,[9] but I don't think he did. Eilert is not a type of a genius—as say Arnold Kramer [10] is—but a young man of great talent—a poet perhaps.

I am unwilling to admit intellectual indebtedness. If an idea is suggested to my mind by another, even though it may seem to me at least very plausible, I oppose it because the suggestion does not come from myself.

Cosgrave and I were looking into Morrow's [11] window one day waiting for Jim. In the window were a number of prints of pictures of young girls at half length and partly undraped. I dislike the window, and about a year before I had remarked to Jim that it reminded me of a butcher's

9. 'Arnold Rubeck is, on the other hand, not intended to be a genius, as perhaps Eljert [sic] Lövberg is' ('Ibsen's New Drama' in Critical Writings of James Joyce, ed. Mason and Ellmann, pp. 65–66).

10. Arnold Kramer is the sensitive young artist driven to suicide in Gerhart Hauptmann's play, Michael Kramer. James Joyce had translated the play into English during his holiday at Mullingar in 1901. James Duffy of 'A Painful Case' makes the same translation; see Dubliners (New York: Viking Press, 1968), p. 108.

11. Booksellers, 12 Nassau St.

shop. On this day Cosgrave said that he did not like the window. I said, 'Nor I. It reminds me of a butcher's shop.' Cosgrave laughed and just then Jim coming round the corner saw him looking into the window and laughing and asked him what he was laughing at. 'I am laughing at these pictures' said Cosgrave. 'Yes,' said Jim, 'they remind me of a butcher's shop.' Cosgrave, of course, immediately concluded that I had repeated as my own what I had heard Jim saying, and looked at me and spluttered out laughing. Cosgrave and Byrne and Gogarty and in fact everybody who knows us is anxious to accuse me of aping Jim, and I suppose Cosgrave thought that here was evident proof. I was foolish enough to tell that I had made the remark to Jim a year before, and Jim admitted it. The best revenge I could have had would have been to let Cosgrave feel happy in the sense of having convicted me. When I had explained, I am sure Cosgrave's opinion of me went up as unjustly as it had gone down.

Gogarty told Jim once that I was an awful thug, that I was grossly affected in manner, a 'washed-out imitation of Jim,' and added that there was only one freak in the family. I admitted that my manner was affected, was a manner in so far as it was affected. Jim agreed and went on to detail how I did not imitate him. As I saw Jim had made up his mind and would believe me only—to use St. Augustine's phrase—'when I confessed unto him,' I said 'Hm.' Cosgrave too thinks I imitate Jim, but these people bore me and I do not care a rambling damn for their opinions good or bad. I really despise them all—Colum, Starkey,[12] Gogarty,

12. James S. Starkey, 'Seumas O'Sullivan', poet and founder of the *Dublin Magazine*.

Byrne, even Cosgrave. I despise them because I cannot do otherwise.

I have read the *Journal to Stella*.[13] It is very uninteresting. I like 'little language', and see possibilities in it for writing, but this journal bored me. The Dean, by the way, remarks playfully to Stella that he would like to whip her a——'for her sauciness,' calls people 'sons of b——s,' invokes 'pox on this' and 'pox on that,' says 'pox on this cold weather, I wish my hand was in the warmest part of your person, young woman; it starves my thigh,' and tells how he is taking a medicine which 'works him' in the morning. Excepting these charming little confidences, the journal is political or scandalous.

Jim has called me brilliant and Cosgrave seems to agree, but I cannot but think them mistaken, perhaps wilfully mistaken. Maybe I think so because I am always conscious of the absence of brilliancy in the manner in which I conceive these ideas which are considered witty. 'My coruscations' come to me slowly and form themselves in my head. Perhaps I am writing. I note them and probably continue writing, and when I have finished I go out trembling with the idea. I am sorry these sayings have been remarked, for I neither wish to be witty—in the ordinary sense—nor to be thought so.

Gladstone is my idea of a great impostor. Jim tells me that the great word in Dante for damning a man is the Italian for 'impostor'. William Ewart Gladstone seems to me to deserve that title thoroughly. The English, with that admiration of theirs in which it is hard to hold the balance between falsity and stupidity, used to call him the Grand

13. By Jonathan Swift.

Old Man, but Parnell's perversion of this is a perfect description of him—a Grand Old Impostor. Parnell must have had a lovely contempt for him. Parnell had, I think, not much ability, except perhaps financial ability; he was not as intimately acquainted with the disadvantages of his country, as say, Davitt, nor knew as well how to remedy them, nor what was most desirable to replace them. He was unlettered, no patriot, and obviously an Anglo-Irishman, but he was a genius and in my judgment the only genius Ireland has produced. He had the power of managing men and using their capabilities, and a great eye for ability. He must have had a very fine mind; he had great words of contempt, 'impostors,' 'peddling.' His genius was probably more distinguished and finer than Napoleon's, but in ambition and ability he was as much the lesser as his success was less than the Corsican's.

Hospitality is not so much a gift as a two-edged pleasure. That was a generous idea of the Italian nobles of the Middle Ages who tried to rival each other in hospitality and prodigality, kept an open table to all comers, and spent large estates in gifts to their dependents.

Jim says that he set out from University College with a few gentlemen of his acquaintance to find his *summmum bonum*. Clancy got as far as McGarvey's.[14]

Aristotle has said that work is a means to leisure, and Coventry Patmore says that all souls in whom there is wisdom hate work. It is probably true that idleness is the first condition of all fine art, and leisure the first condition

14. Cathal McGarvey's tobacco shop in North Frederick St. was a nationalist meeting place, the Cooney's of *Stephen Hero*, Chapter 17. George Clancy is the Madden of that novel.

of all speculation. I am inclined to think that a man should cultivate idleness as far as possible, not any idleness, but his own idleness. Few men are worthy of idleness.

Byrne has the features of the Middle Ages. A pale, square, large-boned face; an aquiline nose with wide nostrils, rather low on his face; a tight-shut, lipless mouth, full of prejudice; brown eyes set wide apart under short thick eyebrows; and a long, narrow forehead surmounted by short, coarse hair brushed up off it like an iron crown. His forehead is lined, and he has a steady look. He is low-sized, square, and powerful looking, and has a strong walk. He dresses in light grey and wears square-toed boots. Jim calls him the Grand Byrne; he has the grand manner, the manner of a Grand Inquisitor. He was born in Wicklow and goes there every summer. My name for him hits the rustic —'Thomas Square-toes.' He is over sceptical as a sign of great wisdom—a doubting Thomas.[15]

The Devil, we are told, fell out of heaven for pride. I guess God Almighty will topple out from stupidity. I offer the opinion that the little old man above had Mephistopheles expelled because he found him too ironical.

I find involuntary emissions, besides being painful in their after-effects, very upsetting. I do not feel physically weaker or ill, but my energy is deranged, my nerves half uncontrolled.

The schismatics from the Irish Theatre objected to Synge's play—a play in which a quick, intelligent peasant woman who has made a loveless marriage is discovered by a trick of her husband's to be intriguing with a young

15. Cf. James Joyce's sketch of Cranly in the opening of Chapter 22 of *Stephen Hero*.

farmer.[16] The old man hunts her out and, the young farmer refusing to take her, she goes off with a tramp while the old man and the young farmer sit down to the remains of a wake that had been prepared. The play is a very good comedy and, with another play [17] also by Synge, is the best thing the Irish National Theatre Society has produced. Naturally, too, it gave better opportunities for acting than any of the other plays gave, and was better acted. But the socialistically moral and free-thinking republicans in Ireland objected to it as a libel on Irish peasantry and Irish peasant life. They seemed to assume—I don't know why—that it was a portrayal of typical Irish peasants, and though they admit adulteries have been committed in Ireland—O thank you Mr. Griffith!—they deny indignantly that adultery is typical.[18] Leaving aside the question as to whether it is more or less typical of Ireland than of Scotland or England or Norway or Germany, do they intend that nothing should be portrayed but statistically observed types? The position may be somewhat unusual, is unusual in as much as it is interesting, but the characters are Irish all of them—the woman, the young farmer, the old man, and the tramp; the humour is Irish and the treatment quite original. Of all the reasons in history or fable for a woman leaving her husband to go off with another man and take the chances of the road, the reason in this seems to me the most comical. She listens, and weighs her chances between going and staying, and at last takes her shawl off a nail and

16. *In the Shadow of the Glen*, first performed 8 October 1903.
17. *Riders to the Sea*, first performed 25 February 1904.
18. Arthur Griffith of the nationalist *United Irishman* had attacked Synge's play as a slur on Irish womanhood.

goes out with the tramp saying, 'Ye've a power o' talk anyway!'

There is sickness in the house. I am the sick one. I am in bed in my own room alone in the evening. Eileen, my white-faced, thoughtless younger sister is playing the 'Rakes of Mallow' on the piano downstairs. I loathe the air. It is a mechanical repetition of the same two or three notes in the same succession, with a turn at the end of each phrase in it to the beginning, like the turn of a handle. She is playing it quickly and badly, stumbling every ten or fifteen seconds, stopping and beginning again. A long string of faces pass slantwise up before my eyes, so quickly that I can hardly distinguish them, but they are grotesque, unhuman, like the faces [19] you see in hucksters' windows painted in cheap yellow paint on cardboard and they are hitched one under the other. I cannot prevent myself seeing them as they fly up noiselessly with interminable length, before my eyes. My palate is quite hard and stiff; everything I touch is stiff and rough. My head is swimming. 'Oh for the Rakes of Mal—low town. Oh for the—. Oh for the Rakes of Mallow town. Oh for the—. Oh for the Rakes of Mal—of Mallow town, the Rakes of Mal—low tow—own.' Damn them, does no one hear me whistling? They won't answer me. I can't whistle whatever—. I wish to Christ someone would stop her—the imbecile! This is intolerable!

The progress of the mind is from doubt to certitude, but how slow has been the progress of what might be called the mind of the world, so slow that it might be doubted whether there was such a thing as progress for it. Its manners, its habits, have changed, the philosophies of the world have no doubt changed, but the world, that Jesus

19. MS note: 'jumping jacks'.

anathemised, has not lost in any marked degree its ancient vice of mundanity nor its stale, fretful dissatisfaction.

I remember reading a passage in S. Augustine in which he blames the pagan poets for making Jove a thunderer and an adulterer. It seems a strangely prejudiced opinion for a man like Augustine to hold. Would it not appear more absurd to make the Holy Ghost a seducer? What fable in Ancient Mythology is more nonsensical than the Christian fable that the three persons are really distinct and equal in all things, equally God, yet not three Gods but one God. Coeval and from eternity, yet Father, Son, and Holy Ghost; the Son begotten of the Father (without a mother, too!), the Holy Ghost by some kind of spiritual sodomy proceeding from the Father and Son (I daren't inquire how). The Father and the Holy Ghost pure spirits and therefore as much above the Son—who is a man, now at any rate—as a man is above a jellyfish. I might very easily catalogue a heap of passions—infamous in the Christian morality—to be found in God: anger, jealousy, revenge, hate and oppression for no reason but to afflict us and try us—possibly damn us. It is amusing that such things should still be believed and seriously argued. But less seriously now, I think, for the day of the different creeds is over.

How happy we unbelievers would be if only Christians would practise a few of their fundamental principles!

Christ's defect was that he was a healer of sick souls; he somewhat distrusted the healthy and he made his religion for the irremediably pathetic. By the bye, who is healthy?

The most demoralizing element of Christianity is the dogma of the Trinity. When taught to children it does the work of original sin, for the making of a contradiction in terms the fundamental belief of a creed has the effect of darkening their understanding in its conception of anything, of puzzling it and of wearying it; and the making of a great sin not to believe firmly in a mystery they can rarely even state to themselves weakens their will and discourages any natural inquiry into whatsoever keeps knocking at their heads. It is easy to foresee that such a training will leave a strong inclination to licentiousness. One child, at least, found it so. I have no patience with those lamentations of saints in temptations to unbelief. Either they had reasons for their beliefs or they had not. If they had reasons surely they must have been convincing reasons. If they had not then they ought to thank their rational intellects for saving them from living in prejudice. Hell and fear is behind it all. They are afraid even to think. One would laugh at the ridiculous idea of Aristotle covering his face with his hands and praying to God in agony of spirit to remove the temptation to disbelieve in the principle that at the same time and in the same connection the same attribute cannot belong and not belong to the same object. What is to be learnt from the saints is not to be learnt from their beliefs but from their spiritual life, and some of the saints in fleeing temptation show that there can be a subtle courage in cowardice.

While I was reading the Confessions of S. Augustine one day, in a somewhat inattentive fashion I came upon these words: 'Are griefs then, too, loved? Verily all desire joy.' B. III, c. 11. The word 'Joy' opened before me like a glory or like an Easter vestment. My eye read on a few lines but I went back and read it—'Verily all desire joy.' It broke upon me, again, mildly springing like a golden and white light. A third time I returned to it, but this time in trying to seize, to remember, to define my impression, I blotted it out altogether. It was a word of three letters connoting something like happiness or comfort or gratification—not joy. It seems to me that many read as I did, vaguely appreciating the reality behind the word, and though they pronounce it distinctly but rarely understanding the significance it has for those that have known joy. I know that this insipidity comes from my lack of spiritual life.

I hate to see Jim limp and pale, with shadows under his watery eyes, loose wet lips, and dank hair. I hate to see him sitting on the edge of a table grinning at his own state. It gets on my nerves to be near him then. Or to see him sucking in his cheeks and his lips, and swallowing spittle in his mouth, and talking in an exhausted husky voice, as if to show how well he can act when drunk, talking about philosophy or poetry not because he likes them at the time but because he remembers that he has a certain character to maintain, that he has to show that he is clever even when drunk, and because he likes to hear himself talking. He likes the novelty of his rôle of dissipated genius. I hate to hear him making speeches, or to be subjected to his obviously and distressingly assumed courteous manner. He is more intolerable in the street, running after every chit with a petticoat on it and making foolish jokes to them in a high weak voice, although he cannot possibly have any desire, his organ of generation being too weak for him to do anything with it but make water. They—the little bitches—run screaming away in pairs and then come back to see if he will chase them again. Jim courts this wasting and fooling although he knows it to be an insinuating danger. He tried it first as an experiment, then he got drunk in company for the want of something more interesting to do. He welcomes drunkenness at times, hoping to find in it some kind of conscious oblivion, and finding I don't know what. Sometimes he becomes quite imbecile, falling up against and mauling whoever he is talking to, or sinks down on the floor quite overcome, moaning and venting huge sighs. Now, however, he gets drunk in the regular way, by lounging from one public house to another. Few things are more intolerable than it is for a sober person to be in company with—it generally means in charge of—a drunken one. Perhaps for this reason I cannot stand drunkards. I hate to see anyone, let him be as stupid as a hog, nine or ten degrees below his standard—drunk; and I know that with time this state becomes permanent.

One of the things that annoys me most about my life in the Church is my silly confessions.

—I eat [*sic*] meat on Christmas Eve.

—Was it at a Protestant house, my child?

—No, father.

— . . . You should never do that, my child. You should never eat meat on holy days . . . days of abstinence. You should always observe the rules of our Holy Mother, the Church. Our Holy Mother, the Church, makes these observances for the good of our souls . . . and eh . . . you should be careful, for the future, always to keep the observances of our Holy Mother, the Church . . . and eh . . . never to eat meat on days of abstinence especially among Protestants . . .

Is there anything else, my child?

I loathe this scene when I remember it. The gradual perception of my stupidity in this and many like acts is like nothing so much as the drawing off of a stocking that has adhered to a sore toe. I wince. It takes my breath away. I loathe myself. I loathe the priest—my ghostly father, my spiritual adviser!— I loathe his little box, his sinnery. And I could so easily have seen my stupidity if only I had let myself! But I was taught to look on priests as a different race.

Voltaire's terror at death exemplifies the fact that if the world talks long enough and loud enough, it can persuade a man of his own evil. He said at one time with a kind of tired wit 'that, after all, he was not so very much worse than the rest of mankind'—so apt we are, if others persist, to take their valuation of us. The belief was beginning to take hold of him then, and it is pitiful to think what he must have believed himself to be in the fever of death. It is small wonder the Church in its inmost heart damns him 'for death,' for he openly damned it 'for life' in France at least.

In this country people are accustomed to confound the name of Dante with the name of Voltaire, and it is not unusual to see signs of pious horror at the mention of Dante's name.

The magnificent lie Eilert Lövberg tells Hedda Gabler to explain the loss—as he thinks—of his manuscript while drunk, is a master-stroke of Ibsen's and is the more effectively used as we have seen Hedda Gabler burning it.

Pappie's religion is the funniest thing about him. He does not conform to it in any one particular, yet he wished to force me to go to mass etc., when I announced my intention of not doing so, and as reports used to come from the College for him to sign, he said he would let the Rector know about me. There was a row about it in the parlour while I was up in my own room reading. I was given to understand that Mother's entreaties had induced him to change his purpose, and that Charlie, who was going in for the Church, had also begged for me, telling Pappie that 'I'd come back.' While the messages were being sent up to me I was highly amused and secretly wishing that Pappie would do as he said (though I knew quite well he couldn't). I was even thinking of 'declaring myself,' as the position would force me to give the priests a taste of my quality, but the final indignity of Charlie begging for me with those words disgusted me. I felt like the dying lion in the fable. The last time Pappie went to Confession and Communion was highly amusing. I bawled laughing at the time. It was about two years ago. Mr. Kane and Mr. Boyd and Mr Chance [1] were to attend a retreat in Gardiner Street, and Pappie, who would never do anything so vulgar from

1. Matthew Kane is the Martin Cunningham of *Dubliners* and *Ulysses*. Charles Chance appears in *Finnegans Wake* and contributed to the character of Bloom in *Ulysses*. (His wife, Marie, contributed to that of Molly.) Boyd is mentioned in *Ulysses*. The incident here recounted was the genesis of the story 'Grace', in *Dubliners*.

himself, was persuaded by Mr. Kane to attend it too. He did so, and came home very drunk for two nights after each sermon. On the second night Chance brought him home. He was to go [to] confession next evening. I heard the conversation down stairs.

Chance. Holy Communion on Sunday morning and then at half five go to renew baptismal vows. They'll give you candles—and then all together we'll—

Pappie (very drunk). Oh, I bar the candles, I bar the candles! I'll do the other job all right, but I bar the candles.

Chance. Oh, that'll do all right—only a formality—but what hour'll we call for you tomorrow night to go to Confession? Matt Kane and Boyd and myself are going at half seven.

Pappie. Oh, I don't know, I don't know—. I'll—. Well, call at half seven then. Will that suit you?

Chance. Splendidly. And you'll come then?

Pappie. Oh yes! Oh yes! Old fellow, I'll go, never you fear, I'll go—. Can you go to whoever you like?

Chance. Oh yes! They've all equal power, all the same.

Pappie. I don't mind, you know. I don't mind, you know. I don't care. I'd go to the first felleh that's open. I haven't got much to tell him, you know. D'you think I have much to tell him?

Mother. I do. God forbid I had as much.

Chance. Oh, that's not the point.

Mother. Oh, no! That's not the point of course.

Chance. It doesn't matter how much you have to tell him, it'll all be wiped off; you'll have a clean sheet.

Pappie. I don't mind, you know. I'd go in to the first

bloody felleh that's open and have a little chat with him. *Chance*. Right! That's right! Now don't forget I'll be here at 5:30.

Pappie went as he promised to Confession on Saturday night and went out early to Holy Communion on Sunday morning. There seems to me to be something irresistibly funny in the picture of Pappie going out at about nine in the morning by himself, trying not to blaspheme about the things not being sent up for him to shave, to go through the farce in the Jesuit Church quite solemnly. I can imagine how much he disliked acting so thoroughly vulgarly. But his vanity would not let this idea remain with him, and he told at the breakfast table (there was a special breakfast on the occasion) how Fr. Vernon [2] (the Jesuit who had conducted the triduum) told him, 'You're not such a bad fellow after all. Ha! ha! ha! ha!' That day after dinner Pappie went to the winding-up lecture at about 4.30 and came home not quite sober with Chance a little before seven. He wanted to borrow money from Mother and was becoming impatient when Mother made a difficulty about giving it, ridiculed her family, and when Mother shook her head at him, went out blaspheming and banging the door behind him. I laughed and said something bitter and satirical. It was certainly the shortest conversion on record. Mother said nothing, but looked patient. *Michaelmas Day* [*1904*]

2. Thus in the MS, but he probably means Fr. John T. Verdon of the Jesuit House in Upper Gardiner St.

Today, Sunday October 2nd, I stood with a number of young men of the lower class, dressed chiefly in navy-blue serge, and wearing hard hats or caps, on the bridge at Jones' Road looking into the Grounds there beside the Canal at a cycle-race. I dislike their flat accents and their interest in sport which fills their Sundays and their holidays. The 'sport' too is vulgar and dull and poor. A cyclist is undistinguished—anyone can be a cyclist. It requires no special ability, no particular training to race as these athletes race. To excel may, perhaps, but it is not in the minds of these young men to excel in anything. I may guess that everyone around me is a cyclist of the same kind as those racing. The racing is a little exciting. The figures move round the course bent jockey-like over the handle-bars. There is a hoarse cheering when they finish, like an enraged acclamation, like a gross oath. Why this brutal excitement? The minds of these men are brutal and low, and the scene like a sketch in crayons by Jack B. Yeats.[1] He seems to like it, but their brutality threatens me—. On Clonliffe Road the browning trees are clear against a pale, cold, blue sky with white puffs of cloud on it, and the sun is bright on the path—. Along the Canal above Dorset Street a man is swimming an Irish terrier. The Canal is steely blue and rippled. The green of the grass is fresh to my eye, the smell of the earth strong—Irish. On the opposite bank at the lock-gates a knot of men are sitting round playing cards

1. Brother of the poet.

—they will play there till evening I suppose. One bursts out with a horselaugh and slaps a card down, the others start arguing and jumping up, talking all together at the top of their voices with cursing and obscenity yet friendly—these are their manners. How can such a pleasure satisfy them! On the Whitworth Road beyond the deep channel where the rail-road runs to my right, a nurse is playing with a black dog in the grounds of the Drumcondra Hospital. I can see she is pretty and young. I would like to be near her, to——. But the wish is impossible. Therefore let it pass. Many people are out, for it is not yet two o'clock, their dinner hour. Before me a tallish young man in a blue-serge suit not new and a hard felt hat is walking with a young woman in a dove-grey costume; obviously she is a bride of some months. I have noticed many brides and many women with child at this time. Is it possible that human beings couple and parturate at seasons, like birds and animals? I hate Sundays—all Sundays, the gentleman's Sunday, the clerk's Sunday, the labourer's Sunday, and worst of all the publican's Sunday. Sunday is the worst day of the week—Dull Sunday. And my Sunday, wherein all the dullness of the week is outdone! That nurse! I would like to lie with her in a bed, now, at mid-day, to see her almost stripped in the daylight. Mid-day lechery! But where's the use of this? Though to be sure mid-day lechery is not unusual. The pungent smell of bleached linen being stretched and asperged with cold water and rolled up before ironing excites to cold bright lechery. Such lechery wears an air of health and frankness but loses in sensual intensity. Something in it dissatisfies me. Sunday dinner, Sunday evening yet to be gone through!

I have examined my face in the glass—naturally without vanity! This is almost a habit of mine, an intention to know my own character as I would a stranger's by criticizing his expression. My head is oval-shaped and rather well capped with a round forehead narrowing a very little at the top and covered with fine, dull-bronze hair, close-cut, with a thread of light here and there in it. My face is square, a little brutally marked at the jaws; my nose somewhat tip-tilted and large, with wide nostrils—sign of sensuality; my chin recedes and my ears, though not large, stand out a little from my skull. My complexion is clean and pale and hollow-cheeked. Under frowning eye-brows, my eyes are large, a dull grey set in clear shining whites. My mouth looks small and is not badly formed in the lips, but the upper lip is deeper than usual, with the downward ridges broad apart and marked, and the corners hidden in a slight droop of flesh. The flesh of my chin is round, with a slight dimple—what is called, I think, an 'artistic chin'. The expression of my eyes is one of steady, soldier-like inquiry, as if it was their duty to examine according to some frowning, meditative morality and to condemn, an expression that remains in them when there is nothing to examine to remind people that they do examine, an affected expression masking real slowness of cerebration. My mouth is surly and tight-shut to conceal the weakness of a character. When the frown lifts, a mind is seen recognising itself without note and without interest, without liking or disliking its own image, a mind which is not pleased yet not consciously displeased because it was born in the ignobility to escape from which it is working and saving up. My face is like Rembrandt as a boy and promises to be like him as a man (or that portrait by him of a man of 37 in a furred busby, which is thought to be of himself) or, when I whistle, like Goldsmith. Gogarty called me Jim's Flemish brother. The background of my mind is as dark as Rembrandt's—without the art, and circumstances can make me as bothered and as foolish as Goldsmith—without the style. My character, what of it there is, is between the two, artist and man of letters. We hear of the minor poet, but who has ever mentioned the minor philosopher. I am he. I am never surprised when anyone dislikes me, nor do I contemn them for doing so, nor attribute it to any jealousy; rather I respect in them the capability of a sudden high judgment. Yet I know it is easier to accuse than to refute. As to my manner, in two words, I have no manner. I wonder what will be thought of me when I lie in my narrow box, with my face of Rembrandt stiff on the white cushions between the edgings of ugly paper-lace! Pitying thoughts—the thoughts I would wish to make impossible. More likely my memory will not be vivid at all. I do not remember my dead vividly. Damn Death anyhow!

Charlie sings like a sentimental policeman.

Jim is thought to be very frank about himself, but his style is such that it might be contended that he confesses in a foreign language—an easier confession than in the vulgar tongue.

I hate the commonplace. I was born amongst it; I belong to it, body and blood. Therefore I hate it. When I think of the commonplace I feel like a scientist who is watching an evil-smelling gas. It repeats in me like a gastric juice. The compact Majority—the Social Monster—is an enemy of all spiritual or intellectual progress and of all emotional purity. Its brutal scepticism is opposed to me. It would have all surrender to its sordidness and accept the maimed, unsatisfying life it insists on. I hate its City life—the chartered life, the love of work for its own sake, the business, the task-work quite contemptible in itself but that by doing it one earns the means to support life. Cities were built to be lived in, not for, and these city-men sacrifice their lives to the City they live in. They have their reward. Paris caused the greatest town in the ancient world to be burnt for his happiness, and modern Europe calls the finest of its cities after him. Pious Aeneas sacrificed his happiness to an admirable sense of duty, and an inconsistent and ungrateful civilisation disregards him. Is there even a hamlet named after him?

The beautiful law of supply and demand is the standard of their valuations and their judgments. The strong law of the survival of the fittest—'fittest' for what? To tolerate life?—galvanizes their existence and their manners. We make our living out of the necessities of others. It is also true that others make their living out of our necessities. But we are gentle, courteous, or commonly civil to others whom we do not like or trust, seldom for the sake of gentleness or courtesy or civility, but that we may win from them the like in return, for only by gentleness can we lay others unwillingly under an obligation. (Through this door enter a Jew carrying a cross.) It is possible, perhaps, that it may be found to be a law of nature that man should have enough work in supplying these necessities to waste his energies, and that philosophy and art are artificial productions, the amusements of idlers, lies, but I have a prejudice that the activity of life is not the obvious thing this seems to make it and the commonplace consider it. There is something false in bright coldness of daylight. There is something defying expression—but perhaps it is in me. How do the work-a-day workers regard these many activities? They do not regard them, they are blindly unhappy. A man is happy in so far as his desires, in the degree of their intensity, are—or in so far as he hopes they will be —satisfied. None but their lowest desires are satisfied, and therefore are they chiefly, vaguely unhappy. The soul is ever seeking its greatest good, and this activity is not their greatest good. Their life is a horrible convulsion between a yawn and a groan.[2] They understand nothing, they are not even aware that there is anything to be understood. They accept civil and moral duties as taxes rightly demanded on freedom and happiness. They are constantly coerced by regulations of Church and State, which regulations being made to restrict freedom were made to be broken. They do not understand their own minds and cannot express themselves, therefore they are unhappy; they are forced by a blind convention into countless acts they have no time to justify to themselves, therefore they are irritable; being unable to express themselves—and we show our knowledge of ourselves, not in what we can say about ourselves (it is rather in what we can say about others, our sentence upon others is our judgment on ourselves) but rather in every act of ours being true to our character—their lives are without style, therefore they are undistinguished and commonplace. It is well to remember that the understanding of the springs of action in others is only guess-work and possibly an illusion. These people may be quite contented.

2. MS note: 'Meredith'.

There is much security in stupidity. But in a number of cases we may believe we are not judging people very much different from ourselves, and we are not mistaken. These people do not seem to be contented. They live like pigs with clerking substituted for grunting. Their lives are crippled from birth like the feet of Chinese ladies. I would like to put them in a novel like 'Les Miserables' and call it 'The Deformed'. The time which the working human race spends in this world may be divided into three parts: the part which is spent in labouring to obtain the means to support life; the part which is spent in renewing or reproducing energy; and the part which is spent in talking about the labour to obtain the means to support life. The ugliness of this life shows itself in their characters, in their amusements, in their laugher, for people betray themselves more in laughter than in drink, not being on their guard against betrayal—*in risu veritas*. It shows in the impurity of their emotions—not corporeal impurity, corruption (though it shows in lewdness, too); corporeal impurity is not the reverse of emotional impurity, is hardly opposed to it in fact; the reverse of this purity is chiefly deceit before men and before oneself. They lie to themselves, and some people who lie to themselves find listeners who believe them. They are full of false prejudices which they endeavour to bear out with empty words, or loud bombast, or the authority of numbers and tradition. And these prejudices like lying tales gather energy in them with every moment of their existence.

In their labouring life they are not admirable, nor are they more pleasing in their Interiors. In their affections they are false, discourteous, gross, and finally overbearing, even brutal. They are capable of perhaps three degrees of sexual affection: common rut, which they appease in various manners but chiefly, when they are newly grown to be men, by fornication; particular rut, which finds an unstable satisfaction in marriage; and the desire for a help-mate, seldom found except in the avaricious, the selfish, the old or the unpleasantly pious. As for their women, they are cowards, probably as great cowards as men but more obviously so, and far more sensual. They want comfort and children, and the more of the former and the less of the latter the better. They really care not a snap of their fingers about anything else. They have the minds of Jews. It is quite beyond their understanding that people should be grievously troubled by the thoughts of their minds. They were the original egoists and from them men have learnt the first principles of a religion which their masculine energy has pushed to such admirable excesses. Naturally, then, the more gracefully selfish they are, the more they are sought. They have a talent for living on the surface and yet being happy. They are foolish, for all their practical wisdom in little things. They are wise in little things be-cause they cannot be convinced of their unimportance. They have not a high kind of intellect and their judg-ments of men and matters are generally valueless, but their impressions are singularly true and they are more impres-sionable even than men. It is a stupid woman who is really deceived in the husband she marries. But they are careful and for all their sensuality they want marriage. The Jew in them wants the bond. That the contract is a fair one, can-not be doubted. They are 'protected' and 'cherished'; they accept the petty, intricate and ceaseless cares of up-bringing children. In chastening a respect which they do not feel from behind into the recalcitrant young they have a labour sufficiently subduing and humiliating for that member, congenial to their heart, and flattering to their lord. He will even stoop to do it himself. Woman's well-implanted sense of duty is very convenient for that constantly preoccupied person, man. Their interior is agreeable to the principles during an armistice, when the active principle has ceased from shouting and smashing chairs and plates, but not so agreeable to the callow human. The youngling is inquisitive and finds much with which he would disagree, and weakness makes him very sensitive of authority. He has a dangerous sense of duties shirked and constant culpability. When parents try to instill into their children's minds the idea that all the duties, all the respect, all the favours and all the gratitude are on one side, their children naturally lose interest in an account where the balance is all on the debtor side and end by repudiating the debt. One would think that the begetting and bringing of children into the world was an act of mortification performed out of a high sense of religious duty. Children are treated as items of domesticity that demand little or no attention beyond the feeding and clothing. They are not supposed to have any privacy, and if they have, as any child with intellectual curiosity or a nature not wholly commonplace but adventurous must have, it is ruthlessly torn open. Coleridge tells in his 'Table-Talk' that when he was a boy at college he came to the conclusion that there was no God. Finding the college unbearable he ran away and went to an old boot maker, told him his story and wanted to be taught his trade. The boot maker was a plain man and did not understand the boy. He brought him back to the college with him to ask the Principal what he ought to do. The Principal abused him roundly for encouraging the boy even so far, and flogged Coleridge. Coleridge said in later life that if he had met that master he would have thanked him for flogging, not arguing. So would I if like Coleridge I wished to believe at all costs in the superstition of a bogey God, for it is well in youth to simulate prejudices in the seat—though not of reason. Similar incidents are referred to in S. Augustine's 'Confessions' but that fine, distinguished and logical intellect speaks exactly contradictory to Coleridge. It must astonish believers to hear him say: 'And if I said [to my soul] "Trust in God", she very rightly obeyed me not, because that most dear friend whom she had lost was, though but human, both truer and better than that phantom in which she was bidden to trust.' Nor does he find, even in idleness, a justification for the punishments he received. He remembers his young days very distinctly and with great bitterness, although he is not a man to complain or write about trifles. 'For this method', he says, 'was commended by our forefathers; and many, passing the same course before us, framed for us weary paths, through which we were compelled to pass, multiplying toil and grief upon the sons of Adam.' And again in the same context: 'Look with pity, Lord, on these things, and deliver us who call upon Thee now; deliver those, too, who call not on Thee yet, that they may call on Thee, and Thou mayst deliver them.' I know many University students of twenty or twenty-one—some of them with their degree—whose letters are opened by their fathers when they go down for their holidays to the country. Patrick McCormick Colm,[3]

3. I.e., Padraic MacCormack Colum.

the Irish messenger-boy genius, the beloved of Yeats and Russell and their clique, and the 'ragged patch' [4] patronized by Millionaire Kelly,[5] has his letters opened for him by his father. At least one Jim sent him was. What kind of courtesy could these *hobble-de-hoys* learn to show their wives when they grow to be men and marry? The average father takes no interest in his sons' education except such as he is made to take by the Commissioner of Education. He does not want them educated. They are afraid to educate them; they would be jealous of their sons. If a boy is being sent to a good college, at least half a dozen friends will warn the father against it. 'He'll become stuck up, I'm telling you, and he'll turn against you.' How often have I heard that from Pappie when, having tried to force his ideals of respectability on Jim and make him enter either for the High Court of Justice or the Bar, he would end by blurting out what he really thought of Jim's ideals—somewhat sensitive then—and Jim by retaliating on Pappie's. Of course Jim can retaliate. They want them trained, taught stock-knowledge, mechanical accuracy. Higher mathematics, even higher arithmetic, is as useless for their pupose as versemaking. More useless, for a good English education makes a man fluent—gives him what they call 'the gift of the gab'. But they say nothing about mathematical studies because, knowing nothing about them, they have a vague idea that they are very intellectual (mathematicians are the stupidest

4. Or him who plays the ragged patch
   To millionaires in Hazelhatch
     —James Joyce, "The Holy Office"
5. Thomas F. Kelly, an American then living at Celbridge, was providing an income for Padraic Colum to encourage Colum's writing. James Joyce had applied to Kelly, without success, for £2,000.

class of men except musicians; they haven't an idea to throw to a dog), very practical, and that anybody who is 'smart at figures' could be a good mathematician if only he could spare the time to study. At most they wish their sons to acquire knowledge, for they know that those that do have a certain marketable value as imparters of the same. What the devil is the use of anybody knowing who killed Julius Caesar any more than of knowing who killed Cock Robin, it occurs to them to ask. They endeavour to engraft their own unreflecting prejudices on the minds of their progeny, and regard objection as disrespect not to be tolerated. The Home is a place where children can learn what their nature chooses from the constant low example of their parents. Yet while themselves living sufficiently disreputable lives, parents demand a high standard of uprightness and virtue in their children, and in at least half a dozen households which I know intimately, if they don't get it their phrase—O irony!—is 'they are no children of mine'. As for trying to understand the character or ambitions of their children, or to help them with advice which is not an empty phrase borrowed from the pulpit—what wisdom have they stored from experience to give—or showing qualities or interests that are either admirable or amiable, the thing is as rare as virtue. Many fathers I know do not know the names of their children. Perhaps there is something we should be thankful for in this ignorance of us when we are at the difficult age, for we want no favours from those secretly unconverted whores who are our fathers. In fine, their fathers are generally the greatest obstacles in children's young life, and the first thing a child has to do on coming to years of discretion is to forget the lies he has been taught. When they are a little grown—say to sixteen or seventeen—the parents have managed (either the one or the other of them—the father for choice) to ruin the household, and they are expected to become sources of income. They feed them indeed, and even this sometimes badly.

Their endeavour to inculcate regular habits in religious duties is entirely ridiculous. Let it pass with a jeer. In their own case I think that, considering unbiasedly Christianity —or in fact any popular religion—we must declare it a failure. For it labours to make the people simple and moral, and to make them love one another—horrible labour—and lay up their treasure in the Next World, but it effects only this, that before they become unconscious at death, men regret a misspent life and sink into hope in the future. A Next World, too, which in the Christian myth is really nothing more dignified than a bogey Court of Justice presided over by an irascible and irresponsible Judge. What little social peace there is, is not due to Christianity, and the justification of Christianity is in those poets who have been moved by its imaginative influences—a poor justification for so dangerous a myth.

But maybe the world has more to say in excuse for its dull life than young philosophers imagine.

I have been reading lately some novels by Henry James and some by George Meredith, and naturally a constant comparison between the two men has been made in my mind. Meredith has the biggest name in English literature today, now that Swinburne has withdrawn, and James has practically no reputation. He is thought to be the writer of patient society novels. In my judgment a stupid injustice has been done to James in this. He is far and away the better novelist, but more than this his work is a much more important contribution to the modern conscience than Meredith's.

Both novelists have the antiquated idea of working out a plot, and their construction is correspondingly bad. In *A Portrait of a Lady*, for instance, he is a trifle prolix and it might justly be objected that unfortunately it is socially impossible to keep an affair such as that between Madame Merle and Osmond, with a very visible result too, such a dead secret and for so long. It is quite unsuspected by the reader and, as an accidental cause being the *deus ex machina* in a psychological novel, is unacceptable. His stories are original and modern and as delicate as his characters, but not always skilful. In *The American*, again there is a surprise sprung on you which nearly spoils the novel. I mean the uprooting of the death of Henri-Urbain de Bellegarde. It is unnecessary to the story, and is neither one thing nor the other between murder and a natural death. More unpardonable still, it necessitates the introduction of a long monologue—another story in fact—and an absolutely undistinguished character—Mrs. Bread. These are big faults but they are less than Meredith's in *Richard Feverel*, where he keeps half a dozen characters working at cross purposes for half the book—about three years. *Richard Feverel* is really three plots: to the end of the Bakewell Comedy, one plot; to the end of the Raynham Courtship, another plot; and the last episode, a third plot. At best it is an old story modernized. *The Egoist* is later and more mature work, but its construction is far worse. It drags intolerably until within about 100 pages of the end, and then ends like a farce by Pinero. He even makes use of a screen and two doors. Four or five unforeseen causes work together to make Crossjay run into a drawing-room and hide beneath a shawl. Sir Willoughby and Letty come in there and talk as they have never talked before, telling one another things both knew quite well for no purpose that one can see except to let Crossjay know all. Crossjay very kindly acts quite out of his character to assist Meredith, and Vernon Whitford and Colonel de Craye evidently know as much about the affair as Meredith himself. There is no other explanation of their conduct. About this latter character the exigencies of his plot make Meredith change his mind at the last moment. Perhaps what is called a 'plot' has little attraction for me, but is seems to me that *The Egoist* has to be written again and that the man who will write it must be able to write without a 'plot', directly from his characters.

Great novelists are chiefly distinguishable from lesser ones by the perfection of their secondary characters. Henry James's secondary characters are sometimes perilously near being boring, but for his Greek sanity of vision and cleverness they would be fatally so. Consider *A Portrait of a Lady*. Lord Warburton is Max Beerbohm's William Archer to the life, a wooden puppet that moves very correctly and wears a beard. Madame Merle is too perfect to have blundered as she did, besides what did she do for all her scheming? She effected what one is led to believe was her purpose, but how? I can explain it only by suspecting that she was in league with James. And then he uses with reference to her a rather caricaturing adjective, the adjective 'large', an adjective which always sprawls over the paper before my eyes into 'la-r-r-rge'. Pansy is pretty but insipid, and Caspar Goodwood intolerably stiff and business-like, a speechlessly earnest person whom James seems to admire. Meredith's secondary characters are better finished, yet I think James has still the advantage of him, for Meredith's manner is, to my thinking, a wrong manner. He treats his marionettes as a jovial god might who had his wine in him. His manner is comic. In every novel there is some character with whom we associate the novelist more closely than with the others. Ralph Touchett in *A Portrait of a Lady*, Adrian Harley in *Richard Feverel*. But Meredith associates himself closely with all, and seems to plead his own excuses by laughing at his creatures. Witness the Baronet, Adrian, Master Ripton Thompson. In Sir Willoughby Patterne Meredith has a chance of achieving something by such a method but it seems to me that he has made him too stupid. Sir Willoughby is less of an egoist and more of a snob than Gilbert Osmond. But it is in delineating women, an art in which Meredith has a reputation, Henry James most shows his superiority. Certainly I know no one to flatter women with Meredith: 'a dainty rogue in porcelain,' 'a dazzling offender,' 'calypso-clad,' 'the ribbons on her dress playing happy mother across her bosom.' But he seems to have no intimacy with the female mind, or if he has he cannot betray it. Few men have. Guy de Maupassant had, it seems to me, and James has, but with a different type of mind. Meredith has done nothing as good as Isabel Archer. Clara Middleton does not compare with her, and Laetitia Dale is almost as boring as Dr. Middlteton. I like Clare Doria Forey, she is a type of invalid beauty, but she is a child. Of James's novels, I think *Daisy Miller* has the least faults. It is a perfect little tragedy of manners. Jim considers Daisy Miller silly, I am sure he is mistaken. I have read it twice and I liked it better the second time than the first. In spite of being apparently a thoughtless, gay flirt, she seems to me to have a subtle and admirable pride and to be very courageous. I like her. It is typical of James's manner that I have absolutely no idea as to whether he approves or disapproves of her. Jim says he cannot understand how any woman could prefer Winterbourne to Giovanelli. Henry James gets phrases sometimes which Meredith could not better. He alludes to Giovanelli as 'the subtle Roman'. Giovanelli knew Daisy Miller far more intimately than Winterbourne and naturally has very good reason not to find fault with her manner. I know he liked her, but he was quite incapable of appreciating her. It is a real psychological catastrophe when Winterbourne, smiling quietly and without any attempt at disguise, decides in his mind about Daisy Miller, so unjustly yet so little suspecting injustice. The only artistic completion of the history is Daisy Miller's death. And James's attitude towards death—a very trying test—is quite without sentimentality. He reproduces the sense of spiritual discomfort at her loss perfectly in his description of Daisy Miller's little grave—'a new protuberance among the April daisies'.

The emotions Henry James chooses to deal with are slight, but in them his psychology is extraordinarily acute and full. He does not put you into the mind of his characters; you always feel you are reading about them, nor does he ever abandon his character of artist to disert upon what he has said—that habit of Meredith's which suggests the psychological essayist (Meredith's psychology always carries its own explanation with it)—but remains patiently impersonal. The Lord be thankit! He is more consistently delicate that Meredith, more delicately humourous, more scientific in treatment, and at least as subtle. He is more finely intellectual than Meredith but not at all as quick or witty. Meredith's wit is chiefly verbal cleverness. He borrows his epigram from his last word, and spoils his psychology with his epigram. He gives the impression of scoring points—not altogether a satisfying impression. His psychology is often laboured, and sometimes no more than an excuse for making his characters act as they do. Meredith thinks with the pen in hand and writes on the spur of the thought. His style is warm with the heat of motion and occasionally a little out of breath. Thinking, it would appear, is becoming an obsolete or at least degenerate science. It is now merely the science of taking notes and putting them together on paper. Of course Meredith is often brilliantly intellectual, but he is a man with a pen and James is not. James writes quietly and without haste and seems to write not what he is thinking but what he has thought. He does not grasp at a thought when it is presented to him, but waits until it has settled itself in his mind's perspective and then arranges it with easy lucidity, writing clearly, minutely, and consequently. James has not the perspicacity of Meredith, but his style has more perspicuity. Therefore his psychology is more readable than Meredith's, because it is not so clearly given. His best style is in his conversations; they are exquisite and marvellous. Meredith's conversations are good, but they are not in the same class with Henry James's. Yet James's conversations are a little too much like fine play between cultivated minds, and again his men and women frequently talk more like people who have lived than like people who are living. His prose style is without colour, for the most part like the writing of an educated gentleman, and at times so wretched as to give the impression that he served his apprenticeship by writing for society papers. It is here that Meredith has the decided advantage over James. James has nothing like Meredith's power over English, or his humour of style, or his force of expression, or his imagination. Meredith is something between a spoiled psychological essayist and a spoiled poet, and though prone to wordiness is one of the makers of English. Meredith in his best passages writes lyrically and can get a magnificent effect by doing so because he can do [it] so well. In *Richard Feverel*, for instance, there is magnificent writing in the chapters 'A diversion on a penny whistle', and 'Clare's diary', in a wood in Germany, and in the second last chapter—in fact all through. During a kindly meant but tedious lecture of the Baronet's to his son, Richard is reminded of Lucy. 'The young man's heart galloped back to Raynham,' says Meredith, and mine galloped back with him. Beside this, the constant urbanity of Henry James's style becomes insipid and lifeless. He seems to have made up his mind to underwrite the emotion, for fear perhaps of being betrayed by the limitations of his nature. The emotion which Jim expresses in:

> Oh hurry over the dark lands
> And run upon the sea.
> The lands and the sea shall not divide us
> My love and me— [6]

6. From 'Go seek her out all courteously', published in *Chamber Music*.

becomes in Henry James 'the zeal of an admirer who on his way down to Rome had stopped neither at Bologna nor at Florence simply because of a certain sentimental impatience.' Besides this he has a really surprising collection of tags: 'inconsequently,' 'with intention,' 'uncultivated minds,' 'always' used for 'still,' 'conspicuous by absence,' things are 'awfully jolly,' and are 'mentioned above,' girls are 'strikingly pretty,' there are even 'pretty men,' he 'tries to sketch scenes,' and addresses his 'reader,' 'at the risk of exciting a somewhat derisive smile on the reader's part—.' His style is frequently absolutely slip-shod and careless, witness the following: 'but the historic atmosphere scientifically considered was no better than a villainous miasma' (*miasma*, Gr. sing., or 'miasm' = an atom or particle arising from putrefying or poisonous bodies; *miasmata*, Gr. plur., or 'miasms', Eng.); and visits at night to the Colosseum, though much valued by the romantics, 'are deprecated by the doctors'. Surely sufficiently bad for a first-rate novelist. But it is in his mind that his style is.

Henry James derives from Richardson through D'Israeli perhaps, and from Goethe, whereas Meredith might be said to derive his mind from Lytton—*The Egoist* labours in the same way as *My Novel*—and from Carlyle, whom his wordiness and rugged writing suggest. My prejudice is that James has the finer tradition. Henry James is the most refined and the most modern writer in modern English Literature. The citizens of his republic seem to have extricated their minds from prejudices and attained an enviable emotional purity, and his treatment of life is consistently a most refined gentleness. His mind, more than any other mind with which I am acquainted, more than Pater's, shows the influence of Goethe. I admire Goethe and I flatter myself that I have a good understanding of his character though I have read very little of what he has written. There are many things in him which lead me to expect that his attitude towards life will supplant in the future that one which Jesus took and the western world has imitated for so many centuries. If he fails to master our world as Jesus and his school did, it will be, I think, because he failed to master himself as they did. His life was chaotic and without order like his work (his lyrics excepted), like his *Faust* and his *Wilhelm Meister*, for in spite of his extraordinary education he is neither in his work nor in his life the artist that Jesus was in his life, yet it seems to me that he will usurp the established power because there is more truth in him. Henry James is his apostle in America and follows him in many things which I find it altogether outside of my power to accept. The affable pleasure and polite interest which Henry James's men and women take in everything and in everybody—an article of the Creed of Goethe—seems to me insincere, because it seems to me that all things and all persons are not interesting and that all things and all persons are not pleasant to meet with, and it seems to me that this habit is disciplinary and an affectation, and that the temper of mind which it produces is unsatisfactory and unsoundly based—a forced growth. I am sure, too, that he enlarges on emotions that Goethe has certainly ridiculed—his Americans' admiration for old monuments for instance. In *Daisy Miller* Winterbourne, visiting the Colosseum in the luminous dusk of the moon, is made to walk up it with his coat-collar up reciting Byron's 'well-known lines' on it. This is that horrible sentimentality that spoils *Werther*, the

Goethe that Goethe laughed at. Henry James is so safe behind his style that I would have suspected him of laughing
at Winterbourne but that this sentimentality for the historic
and the picturesque re-occurs constantly in his novels. I
have other quarrels with him than these. The men and
women who are the protagonists of his stories are, we may
assume, not Christians, nor are they believers in any deistic
religion, yet they rule their lives according to a certain
morality. It would interest me to know what they mean by
'morality', and on what in reason they base their 'sense of
duty', 'sense of honour', and 'sense of privacy'. Caspar
Goodwood and Henrietta Stackpole are types of pious
members of the religion of America, and to my thinking
they are quite hopeless. They are as full of prejudices as
my father, the only difference being that their prejudices
are newer. Nearly all novelists have their pet prejudices,
which I find objectionable. Meredith has two that are constant and that I remember. Vernon Whitford is one. He is
the muscular young Englishman who expels nonsense and
induces uprightness of spirit by long-distance walking.
But perhaps like Shelley's Indian lover he has 'a spirit in his
feet'. Meredith's admiration for the lean of meat—in writers a mark generally of those who in spite of intellect have
a weakness in them of which they are conscious and a
brutality of which they are not—is excelled only by Sir
A. Conan Doyle's adoration of prize-fighters. This admiration is a different thing from Michael Angelo's body-
worship, which is mainly the worship of formal beauty,
it is not even the worship of athletic beauty—there is
nothing athletic in such heaviness—it is the carnal stupidity of what I have named to myself the cyclist mind. There

is danger that these people really prefer their bodies, and when their minds prefer their bodies to their minds, all men of sense must agree that they are right. I have noticed however—observing the crowds who come down to swim at the Bull Wall—that their commonplaceness is as easily detected in their bodies as in their eyes. By the way, women hate big men of muscle. Meredith's other stupidity is his idea about boys. He thinks that all boys have to do is to tell no lies, eat pudding, and get birched. The birching, he says, will cure morbid sensitiveness.

(*By the bye*, that reminds me. I remember many years ago at Belvedere a young boy mitched and was found out. A Jesuit named Fr. Ryan [7] did the flogging then, and it was in his class the boy was. Ryan flogged him in the morning. Afterwards at lunch time Ryan came over to him in the class-room, smiling and playful. Ryan seldom smiled and was never playful. 'So you stayed away because you were afraid of me,' said he, and began tickling the boy till he wiggled out of him and ran away. Ryan's complexion was pale with a blueish chin. He became red. *Mem.* This incident is not supposed to have any meaning.)

The occupation of boys, according to Meredith, is to be outdoor sports, for it is one of the principles of moral hygienics that these expel suprapatellar [8] curiosities. I cannot imagine how these simpletons expect football to vie in attractiveness with the weak loins of young girls and their white next linen warm with the flesh, except by supposing that they became elderly men at a jump, without ever pass-

7. Fr. Francis Ryan, who taught French and Italian. He is mentioned in 'An Encounter', in *Dubliners*.

8. I.e., above the knees.

ing through the restrained and perverted lechery of puberty. Meredith, to be sure, alludes to the 'apple season' (Jim did not understand this to refer to the Adam and Eve affair till I reminded him), and this is so delightfully witty that one can forgive him any amount of stupidity for it, but on the whole I think his prejudices are more stupid than James's.

A certain asexuality is over Henry James's men and women, and perhaps for this reason he is not at all comparable to Meredith as a poet nor is he ever the lover Meredith is. He totally disregards what certain French comic papers supply so well and with so little shyness. He does not allude except in rare and distant phrases to the self-insistent difference of sex, and his men and women might be accused of waxing too dainty for their uses. 'Many of these' delectable impressions, he writes, 'still linger in the minds of our travellers, attended by a train of harmonious images, images of brilliant mornings on lawns or piazzas that overlook the sea, innumerable pretty girls, infinite lounging and talking and laughing and flirting and lunching and dining'—but that is just the point. I opine that it is impossible for sensitive males to treat girls as if they were pretty tea-cups. He fails to interest me in this summer holiday life. Pretty, confined, ineffectual, is the life he shows at Newport; I feel like Gulliver among the Lilliputians when I look down on it. He is far more irreligious than Meredith. Meredith talks a little too much about God. God is so hidden that what can be said about him belongs to philosophy. What Meredith has to say about our first cause is not of this kind. It is most unpardonable sentimentality about an old gentleman in a beard, who lives in heaven and is very much like his grandpapa. There is nothing like this in James. He satirizes the religious beliefs with his usual temperate urbanity. It is hard to believe that he is quite serious when writing in *The American*, describing young de Bellegarde's death, he says the door was opened for someone to come in. 'This was M. le Curé, who carried in his hand an object unknown to Newman and covered with a white napkin.' Or in *Daisy Miller*, ' "My father ain't in Europe, my father's in a better place than Europe." Winterbourne imagined for a moment that this was the manner in which the child had been taught to intimate that Mr. Miller had been removed to the sphere of celestial rewards. But Randolph immediately added, "My father is in Schenectady." ' He writes more seriously of a French gentleman of an old family, '*Savoir-vivre*—knowing how to live—was his speciality, in which he included knowing how to die, but as Newman reflected with a good deal of dumb irritation, he seemed disposed to delegate to others the application of his learning on this point'. Henry James's mind is socialistic; there are years of sanely reasoned disapproval behind the convent episode in *A Portrait of a Lady*. Writing of a nun's voice, he says, 'It fell with a leaden weight upon Isabel's ears; it seemed to represent the surrender of a personality, the authority of a Church'. Henry James does not mention any other church but the Catholic Church that I know of; he seems to take it because it is the old feudal Church, the traditional Church, the aristocratic Church which is most uncompromisingly monarchical. We get nearer his personal opinion of it with Newman in *The American*. At Mass in the Convent Chapel where Madame de Cintré has been immured 'Newman watched their genuflections and gyrations with a grim, still enmity; they seemed aids and abettors of Madame de Cintré's desertion; they were mouthing and droning out their triumph— (a wailing sound). It was the chant of the Carmelite nuns, their only human utterance. It was their dirge over their buried affections—. It was horrible; as it continued Newman felt that he needed all his self-control. He was growing more agitated, he felt tears in his eyes. At last, as in its free force the thought came to him that this confused, impersonal wail was all he or the world she had deserted should ever hear of the voice he had found so sweet, he felt that he could bear it no longer. He rose abruptly and made his way out'. The emotion Meredith harps loudly on is love, in Henry James it is freedom. Sentences remind one of freedom with a thrill. They show an unusual and fine courage in their use of their freedom, yet there seems to be some horrible paralysis in them at crises. These Americans seem to regard their nation as an experiment of the result of which they were rather proud, and freedom as their national religion. The American girls seem to be even more conscious of their birthright than American men; they demand and use an emotional and conventional freedom when their men are working for politic. I do not understand their idea about flirting and their offence when love is mentioned. If they think that friendship and intimacy with men is possible without desire, they deceive themselves. They have great courage to make the experiment when they come to Europe in the face of convention and with such thoroughness, but they succeed only because of a defiant spirit. I do not know what satisfaction they get out of such a Pyrrhic victory. But it seems to me, if one may trust Henry James, that America has more to expect from her women than from her men. Compared with Tolstoy or Turgeniev neither Henry James nor Meredith has very much to say. Neither could have conceived *Master and Man.*

'Billy Byrne' is a fine threatening air.

I am pestered with dogs and children while I am writing with my window open. I wonder how no one has written to the papers about the dogs in Cabra Park. They bark all day and the greater part of the night. If one were sick this would be intolerable. I hate noise just as I hate stinks, yet I have endured three dogs answering each other from back-yards, and children 'la-la-oo-ing' for hours on end. It is one of the secret improbable desires of my heart to shoot the dog next door. Dogs and children reject very accurately the household in which they were reared.

[*13 October 1904*]

When my mind is unsettled old men like Pat Casey [1] irritate me. They say the very things my mind quarrels with, while from politeness I must listen to them, and from listening must appear to acquiesce.

Pappie had borrowed 2l. from Temple, proprietor of 'The Hut',[2] had stood drinks and had been talking old times for an hour, and now, waiting outside the public-house for him, Pat Casey was shaking my hand. He held my hand

1. See p. 134, n. 4, below.
2. Hugh Temple's grocery and spirits shop at 157 Phibsborough Rd.

and seemed to catch some of my restlessness for he kept glancing shiftily at a gable-end opposite and mumbled awkwardly:

Good-bye—a—a—good-bye, my dear boy—and—a—a take care of your father, now that James is gone away [3] —don't let anything separate you—you don't mind me— as an old man—a—a—to a young one—I know—a—a— my dear boy—I know—a—a—your father loves you all —he has gone through a great deal of trouble—and you ought to take care of him, my dear boy—and—a—a— please God—please God you all be happy—good-bye now my dear boy——

and the rest of it, in a thick brogue.

Knowing the immediate cause of the advice—drinks and the stories, Pat Casey's own struggles with poverty—and the temper of mind in which it was given to me, I was acutely bored. I kept smiling and moving on my feet and saying 'Oh yes', and 'Of course', and 'Not at all', and 'Good-bye'. If there is anything more boring than being bored, it is being bored and trying to appear interested. I was restless and, like a boy being flogged, was telling myself that this infliction could not in reason last much longer. I was not even surprised at the bare-facedness of the platitude till I had left him. The expression was trivial and vague, the expression of a trivial and vague mind, but the intent was grave to me and I did not agree with it yet could not securely put it aside.[4] My treatment of Pappie with dis-

3. James and Nora had sailed from Dublin on 8 October.
4. MS note: 'Besides, Pat Casey (called "of Paris") is an old man of a few settled ideas, in secret an unbeliever (I believe) like myself, and a man who has lived abroad for fenian complicity.'

like would be cried out upon by men of this kind, disapproved by Jim, and not approved by myself, because my dislike of him has shown itself, though indeed rarely, unstable. Besides, I admire those who treat their fathers with respect, though I know that honouring one's father is a subtle way of honouring oneself. I do not like being near Pappie and when I ask myself why, I cannot pretend to like him. How much I am dependent upon the minds of others, and how much I dislike the fossilized stupidity of old men! I avoid Pat Casey in the street, and dislike him in the manner of loathing, though he professes to like me very much. I am sorry for it.

I am often conscious of suspending unfavourable judgment on people all the while I am speaking to them.

Listening in silence to another eating is most unpleasant.

The world is full of a number of things that I do not understand, and I am insufferably wearied by Reviews and Magazines because they remind me of them, and because I can plainly see that the contributors do not understand them any more than I but write from the point of view of the latest catch-word. Besides, the style of these articles is generally wretched. The contributors all seem to desire to write finely or picturesquely, and these desires are perhaps the greatest foes to style.

I like idling but I hate being kept idle.

This pain is the grossest tyranny of Nature. I walk with little steps along the asphalt, treading on the outside edges of my feet, for an iron rod of pain transfixes my bowels and they emit burning gas. The people flit past me on the roadway. The scales seem to have fallen from my eyes, and I see them with the unnatural clearness of the sick. They do not seem like human figures; their bodies seem imponderable, and they pass not with a motion of their own but like daylight ghosts, out of my tense and hurried vision. The noise of a coal-cart passing near me with shaking bell crashes in upon my ear. I turn all hot. I am suffocating. In a moment I shall cry out to them. No, I shall not even grunt—. The pain begins slowly to weaken. I turn all cold. Now this is pleasant, for the loosening of sharp pain is one of the pleasantest of experiences—a Platonic pleasure. I almost forget now the pain my body had but a few seconds ago, for the memory of the senses is short, except that a dull fire remains in me and that it has left me trembling. It will come again, but how soon? In how many seconds? In thirty seconds? In a minute? How many times before I reach home? It is coming again, and I am almost running from it as if it were chasing me, not in me.

I have read Kipling's *Plain Tales from the Hills*. It is the first book of Kipling's I have read and I am greatly disappointed. I conclude it takes far more talent to write remarkable short stories than to write a good novel, for I have noticed that many good novelists fail in the short story. Kipling's mind is quite commonplace, like Mick Manning's of *The Herald* or like Pappie's, but clever. It is that type of mind which has a strong sense of the actualities of common sense and of convention, and is as unpleasant as these. The stories are wretchedly written in a half-comic, half-satirical, conversational style. His point of view is one of married shrewdness. He seems to wish to impress on his reader: 'I am older than these young fellows I write about, and I've seen a bit more of the world than they did and I know the ropes. I was young and had those ideas myself at one time, but in the long run the commonsense view is the right way of looking at things.' The collection is of anecdotes, not of tales. They remind me of Pappie's reminiscent anecdotes. Like him, Kipling always tells you how many rupees a month his hero had, what was his business, and whether he was a smart man at it. But Pappie tells you his appearance and proportions, and imitates his manner and his voice, or burlesques them. Kipling moralizes on his tales with one eye shut. 'There are more ways of running a horse to suit your book than pulling his neck off in the straight. Which everybody knows. But you couldn't tell so-and-so that. He knew too much. I knew a fellow once—but that is another story—. One night the crash came. As was quite natural. When the trouble was over etc.'

His style is as conversational as this. He talks a little too much about horses to please me.

> ' "Stopped in the straight when the race was his own!
>   Look at him cutting—cur to the bone!"
> Ask, ere the youngster be rated and chidden,
> What did he carry and how was he ridden?
> May be they used him too much at the start,
> May be Fate's weight-cloths were breaking his heart.'
>   *Life's Handicap*

His horsey sentimentality draws tears from people of Pappie's mind, is very English, and pleases Englishmen. One or two are tales (the title is the best thing in the book). I like a little of 'Beyond the Pale', but it ends like the rest in anecdotive chat. I believe Moore has compared his use of English to Shakespeare's. I am astonished. I suspect Moore did so because he had to look out so many slang terms and Anglo-Indian words in a dictionary.

I was paid a fine compliment by a drunken man. He told

me he had met me before with Pappie and asked me had I travelled much. I said I had never travelled at all. He seemed very much surprised and said he thought I had lived a long time away on the Continent. I tried to persuade him that he was mistaking me for Jim. But he stuck to his point with the persistence of a drunken man who remembers only one thing. He said he knew Jim well and that Pappie had told him that he had been a couple of times in Paris, so I gave in and asked him what made him think I had travelled—my accent? 'Ah, no—your manner. I thought from your manner that you had travelled a share.' Jaysus! My manner! For once in my life a drunken man interested me. The compliment was the finer as I am quite sure it was not intended.

[December 1904]

It is now December and for this year we have lived in this house on practically starvation rations. There has been a very small breakfast, perhaps, no dinner, and no tea, and at about seven o'clock I find the house intolerable and go down town. Very frequently I meet on these strolls fellows who were in class with me in Belvedere coming home from business. They are, evidently, useful members of the community since they are worth being paid. I am, in a word, an idler, or if you prefer, a wastrel. I am living on the very meagre fare of idleness, and am at present very conscious of its insufficiency, while I amuse myself picturing the domestic security to which they are returning—fruit of industry. They are believers; I am an unbeliever. I remember the trite moral the vulgarian priests who were my masters, the Jesuits, would draw from my case. My mind must be very lax and my thoughts very desultory, for I permit myself to think lazily and quite without sincerity, would I change with them? I am not over-clever but I am not stupid. I could easily cultivate the domestic virtues, throw up the sponge, and become a not-commonplace citizen. What in the end am I trying to do with this head-piece of mine? But if my mind has been lax, it suddenly rises up and is glad, for I would not change with them. I have no certitude in me. If they are right, then I lose all. If I am right, they certainly suffer nothing. I quite envisage the fact that my policy is bad policy, but I could not change with them if I would. I can answer them no questions, but I do not believe their blessed fable of Jesus Christ nor in the Church they have built out of it, and though I am quite without principles and accuse myself of inconsistency, a personal honour will not let me try to believe for policy's sake. This enlivening of my faith in unbelief seems to me not unworthy. They stop me (because they regard me as an amusing fellow, I think) for I rarely stop to speak to any one of them. A gawky idiot legs it up to me slowly, with a broad grin on his face. I would have preferred to nod and pass on. However (as Pappie would say), I find myself talking as if I were repeating the lines of a role, mechanically twisting and turning phrases.

—Hello, Joyce.

—Hello, Dodd. How are you getting on? Are you studying hard for your exams these times?

—Yes. But not too hard, you know. (*With a significant laugh to me.*) I've two more chances.

—Oh I see! Just hard enough to fail?

—Yes. (*Laughs.*)

—With honour?

—Oh! with honour, of course! (*Laughs.*)

—I see. Oh, that's right. So long.

Ugh! The Thing! The Fool! The Imbecile! Did you see him chuckling in his long neck with delight at being let live? The bloody ostrich!

Some women approach love after marriage. Mother, I think, was one of that number.

Jim read these Notes of mine when he came back into the house.[1] He threw them down without a word. He cursed me in jest for not having written anything about himself and Nora in them, and later amused himself by parodying them. His parody was something like 'Sometimes I do be thinkin', goin' along the road, etc.'

Ruskin said, I believe, that the true test of a man and what he believed in would be what he would do if he were told that he would be dead in a few hours. The vulgarian priests like this rubbish but I prefer a reply St. Stanislaus gave. One day he was sent out to play ball with the other novices. While they were playing, one of the novices asked him what he would do if he were told he was to die in an hour. 'I would go on playing ball,' said St. Stanislaus. I do not like this insipid little saint, but on this occasion he seems to me to have cerebrated with great distinction.

Jim turned a number of the Irish literary clique against him by announcing his dislike for work and his intention to do it only when he must, whereas Colum is highest in

1. That is, after 19 September, when he returned home to St. Peter's Terrace after having lodged elsewhere during the summer.

their favour because he is a strenuous little poet, and writes strenuous poems. These people forget that Jim's idleness is of more importance than Colum's work, because Jim is never idle except when studying for an exam, but always spiritually very much alive.

I shall call these Notes 'My Crucible', because I try to refine myself in them and to separate what is subtle from what is gross.

When Charlie is going out in the evening Pappie starts, 'Where are ye going, Ch-a-a-arlie? Down to the Murrays, I hope'—and the rest of it. 'Going down to sponge on them for porter, eh? Sucking porter, that's all you're good for. You seem to be very fond of them. Ye'll get out of this, ye bloody waster of hell. Ye can go and stay with the Murrays, then. Ye can go and sponge on them as your brother did'; and much more. Charlie takes no notice of him, but goes out. He never goes down to the Murrays, but I go every night almost. I feel very cowardly while this is going on, though I don't see how I could help it. When Pappie asks me where I am going, which he does sometimes, very apologetically, I say 'Out,' or sometimes 'Down town'. I never asked myself where he thought I was going, but I had a vague impression that he knew very well. I left Pappie once or twice in the street to wait for me while I went to talk to Aunt Josephine at Aughrim Street. I think it was noticeable that I showed myself very different from him towards any members of the family that called up. When Jim Murray was diffident about going into the room where Pappie was, I went in with him and affected more intimacy with him than, I think, exists, and would have affected more but for fear of appearing patronizing, and finally I left Pappie (who was fairly drunk—his most abusive stage) to come home by himself, so that I could go and see Katsy home, very sincerely and much preferring her society to Pappie's. I have to his knowledge received presents from both Aunt Josephine and Katsy, yet I must suppose that all this was wasted on him for he never abuses me about them. I thought once or twice that his abuse of Charlie was meant for me, but the other day he said he hoped I wasn't in with those blackguard friends of Jim's. I said I hadn't seen any of them for months. Pappie may have been play-acting, pretending to think that I went to them every night I went out, so as to lead me to believe he did not know I went down so constantly to the North Strand.[2] Anything is possible with Pappie. If he does not abuse me, although he would like to, it is because my tongue and my temper are at least the equal of his; but if he is really deceived then he is too stupid and too blind to observe what is quite plain to others. I have never found him either stupid or blind. I have thought I should say, 'I have reason to know Charlie does not go to Murrays as I go down there constantly and he is never there,' but this would seem to me, somehow, like an explanation, and would stick in my throat. His abusing Charlie for sponging may, all unknown to me, have something to do with my unwillingness to accept drink from Aunt Josephine. I get over my unwillingness pretty frequently, sure. Yet when one is so full of doubt and indecision as I am, little causes have inordinate effects.

Pappie has had a rather Byronic education, being the only child of an only child and spendthrift, and being left to be educated by an elderly, sulky, and uncertain-

2. Where the Murrays lived at No. 103.

142

tempered mother. Lately in the evenings when I go down to Fairview, I have desisted during my walks with Aunt Josephine and Katsy from my attempt to utter no words but revised wisdom. I have begun to talk a great deal, in fact, and mostly about Pappie, until one night Katsy with her usual sharpness and impudence told me in fun, 'Oh, that'll do, John. Don't talk so much about your "ould fellah".' I had an impression that she had the right of me again, and this, with the knowledge that I was caught in a false position, somewhat annoyed me. I concealed my annoyance, however, by fondling her, for I have learnt to conceal my annoyance, and, I suspect, been taught to try. I have not a particle of affection for Pappie, yet I do not think I underrate him. Nor do I think I overrate him. What I had been telling about him were accomplished facts. I know that he has made something out of his life and has enjoyed himself in a way. I have been watching him in many phases, watching him drunk, watching him sober, watching him when he has money and when he has not, when he is on friendly terms with me and when he is not, and as a result I find I do not like him. I think it very likely, now, that from this forward I shall take less notice of him. I wrote once that I disliked Jim,[3] but I see now how I was led to believe a lie. With reference to anyone whom we know, we may like or dislike more than one thing; we may like that person's character, for instance, and yet dislike what he does or the way he does it. Jim had done many things which I disliked and had slighted me a few times before I wrote. Now that I think of it, I suggest I may have been irritated by the demands which,

3. See p. 50.

quite unknown to me, Jim's presence made on my character; but more than all this, the idea of affection between characters so distrustful and mutually so little affectionate repelled me as it does now. I think I understand Jim, however, and like him in the way of admiration. As for my interest in Jim, it has become chronic, for it has always been my habit to try to live Jim's intellectual life as well as my own.

I am glad I have written a kind of appreciation of Henry James, because I dislike him very much. My admiration of him was one of those peculiar admirations, like Edgar Allan Poe's admiration of Lord Tennyson, which are forced upon you because you understand the person so well, while for exactly the same reason you cannot give him all the honour in your mind. I think I understand Henry James very well because of a certain similarity of character, and, for this same reason disliking him, I have perhaps overrated him for fear I should underrate him. So, too, when Poe said Tennyson was the greatest poet that ever lived he did not quite believe what he said, and therefore repeated it in italics. He admired Tennyson very much in this forced way and risked the statement hoping that if Tennyson should be considered a very great poet by his posterity—say as great as Shakespeare is considered—people would say of Poe, 'What a discerning critic! And to declare it while Tennyson was still alive! So difficult!' Unfortunately for Poe's memory, posterity does not seem in any hurry to exalt Tennyson.

I think when men get drunk what they most display is their vanity, their ugly and stupid vanity, their prodigious vanity.

I have a new idea for a honeymoon; that the happy couple should get into bed and stay there for a week, getting their meals brought to them.

Tolstoy's return to Nature and simplicity is so much less than Rousseau's as a conviction is less than a passion. I once thought Tolstoy very intellectual, I now think him only clever. Unlike Saul, the son of Kish, Tolstoy seems to me to have gone out to find a kingdom and to have found his father's asses.

I am displeased with these notes because I know that every thought of my mind is not interesting of itself, yet I am irritated when I cannot articulate every disordered and inconsequent thought of it, because I seem to have the idea that they will be of interest experimentally.

I taught Jim two things, to whistle and to curse.

There is a legend that when Christ was born a voice was heard in Greece saying, 'Great Pan is dead.' D'Annunzio proclaims, 'Great Pan is not dead,' but I suggest that Christ is.

I have read the *Decameron* of Giovanni Boccaccio twice completely through, and many novels from it much oftener at times when I had a mind for lecherous reading. Now on my last reading I dislike them because the pleasure is not subtle enough for me, I think. To tell the truth, they never excited me much, I never regarded them as lecherous tales. What chiefly held my attention was the manner of telling and the kind of life they portrayed. I had read them in an English translation (though in one story they thought it more decent to give a page of French) and of course the style is translation English. I like some of the tales well, some even very well; some are witty, often he gives a witty turn to the story; I admire the picture of Italian life he gives in some, and the freedom of the natural soul that is in all; but after a hundred stories I think that the book is wretched. They remind me of a saying of Paracelsus. Paracelsus said that the artist must do nothing but separate what is subtle from what is gross, what is pure from what is impure. In a sense it might be said that Boccaccio did this, but that he kept the wrong retort. Yet I like very well those stories which are catalogued in booksellers' lists under the title 'Erotic'—when they are well told, when, in fact, they are by de Maupassant.

I like instrumental music best, better than songs, better than operas, and this seems to me strange as I have absolutely no knowledge of music or of any instrument, and not much ear. I am very hard to please in operas, perhaps because my ear is confused. I generally look at the shoulders of the people under me so as not to see the acting. Operas seem to me literally screaming farces, and I like best those that are simple or those in which the melody is strange. I have no love for orchestration, and when it makes the voice difficult to hear I abominate it. I consider it chiefly (when, that is, it is not playing by itself) as an accompaniment to the singer. I suspect that this is very vulgar, and that in Wagner, for instance, the orchestration is frightfully intellectual, but then I prefer a rich voice to an intellectual singer. In waltzes, polkas, mazurkas, chacones, nocturnes, fugues, bourrées, sonatas, and even overtures, I take a very genuine pleasure.

People like Jim easily, although he is a man of strange impulses. Perhaps it is because he is so much alive. He seemed to me the person in Ireland who was most alive.

My own want of energy, of what they call 'heart', oppresses me. I remind myself of de Goncourt's saying about Saint-Beuve, 'that he was always gnashing his teeth in disgust that he was not a handsome young officer of hussars'.

Tommy Moore and Waldteufel [4] are the two most typical poets of the common mind, I have heard, and just as Moore has written one or two poems, Waldteufel has written one or two waltzes.

[*January 1905*]

It is now January 1905 and I am still writing at these notes. I dislike them very much. They are not honest. I have often determined to burn them and write no more, but for the sake of some things well-expressed in them have spared them. They are to any shrewd reader the workings of a worthless mind with nothing beautiful in it. Yet now, envisaging a new-discovered vice of dishonourableness, I am preparing to continue them because of my habit of idleness and my silent egoism, although I do not hope to set down anything in them that will please me, for my life is now, even more than formerly, like a stale taste and emptiness in my mouth. I have been dishonourable. This word shames me yet it shouldn't, for I have no standards of conduct and no principles. When Aunt Josephine once told me (to prove to me that Uncle Willie liked me) that he had said to her that I 'was a lad who had some principles but that Jim had none', I was not pleased, knowing the elements of cowardice, indecision and prejudice of which

4. Emile Waldteufel (1837–1915), French composer.

these 'principles' were compounded, and I pictured how narrow my life would become inside them, and how much pleasure I would have to deny myself for the ignoble and inconsistent end of earning the praise. When Jim was told, he seemed to take it as a compliment, at least to his consistency. Now when I am expecting to hear that I have none, I feel still ignoble. I am hard to flatter, certainly. Jim is none so difficult to flatter, for I suspect that if I wrote to him 'after all, you have both honour and peculiar principles of your own' (which, by the bye, is hardly more than truth), he would take it as a compliment again. With regard to these notes, I have noticed that the later ones are better written, so that perhaps by writing them I am learning to write. Once or twice I have been able to say, looking at parts in it, 'That's good.'

Jim's criticisms of these notes of mine are characteristic. One of them is this: 'An' do ye be sittin' up here, scratchin' your arse, an' writin' thim things.' He pronounces 'arse' something like 'ærse'.

Some people say, 'You can never know what you can do until you try,' but it seems to me that I can never know what I am able to do until a twelvemonth after I have done it.

I am tempted seven times a day to burn these notes. I yielded to the temptation in summer, 1903, and burnt a long and full diary which I had kept for two years. Jim said he was very sorry I burnt it, as it would have been of great use to him in writing his novel, [1] and if it would have

---

1. James asked for the use of the present diary, too, writing from Pola on 13 January: 'Send me all documents dealing with University College from your diary &c' (*Letters of James Joyce*, ed. Richard Ellmann [New York: Viking Press, 1966], II, 76).

been of use, I am sorry too. Aunt Josephine, who was staying in the house at the time, asked me not to burn it, but I did so to make myself believe I was burning my ships. I shall probably not burn these, however, as Aunt Josephine has repeatedly asked me to give them to her when I want them no longer. I would give them but that looking through them I find that they are very ugly and I would be shamed if they were found in her drawer. But it is sure that I shall not keep them, for I find that few things are heavier to have on your hands (or on your conscience) than paper that has been written on.

The rabblement of this country have a fondness for the dock. Their patriots have posed like virtuous servants before their unvirtuous masters and made speeches from the dock. This form of distinction is much admired by the vulgar, and in 'Christ before Pilate' it is—with the merely brute appeal of a scourged back in 'Ecce Homo' too, perhaps—the only element of vulgarity which its narrators have introduced into the legend of Jesus Christ.

It has hitherto been given as a sufficient reason for not sinning that it offends God, who is good in himself. Such a reason is obviously insufficient and impotent, and only belief in Hell has held the people in check. The justification of morality must be found in the nature of the acts themselves, and I would not be surprised if morality had not any philosophical justification, and were to make what apology it could from temperament and refinement.

The chief thing I found when I left the Church was that 'ugly little beast', a conscience. Rather I won it, for it is quite true that the Confessional is a 'conscience bank', and that its directors keep a marvellous tight grip on their capital. Besides, Confession and Penance, which are in a way the chastisement of sin, kill the conscience, because chastisement is expiation and kills the acuteness of one's sense of the wrong consummated, but it humiliates and emphasises one's vague sense of having done wrong. So long as any governing body has the authority to tell you what you shall consider either right or wrong, your conscience is not your own. It is uncomfortable, however, for the free conscience to be unable to blame anybody but itself and to be forced to regard every act in the past of which it disapproves as indelible.

I have reckoned about half a hundred of Ireland's pet cattle of the square mile. They are sleek and well-fed, ungolden calves, fatted calves. Perhaps they are worshipped because they are the idols of Ireland's national vices. I do not like priests, but I think I like nuns even less. Nuns seem to me women who want one thing but try to want another. Forced purity is as horrible to me as a nagging tongue or a scraggy body or a shrill voice because I like sensuality when it is neither gross nor stupid. I seem to think that all purity is constrained but that men carry it better than women, having so many other interests. Women may have other interests to be sure; this is the judgment of a male, and perhaps I am like the psychological novelists who, remembering their weaknesses, portray them in women. Men are delighted and women wonder. I have no love for purity anyhow, and never had. The May hymns always seemed to me good aphrodisiacs. I think I shall marry a Jewess, for they seem to me the only people who have a plausible theory of chastity and sexuality.

I abhor old age.

A woman's love never brooks the delay of sacrament,

for as the woman's desire is for the man's desire, the woman obtains her desire before marriage, and what she gives in marriage is a kind of reward or consummation. I have written 'what she gives'; who would ever speak in this connection of the man 'giving'? Nevertheless marriage means more for a woman than for a man, for whereas a woman enters into the fullness of life by marriage, a man gives hostages to fortune. Marriage is a 'becoming' something, a 'setting up' for the woman, but a 'settling down' for the man. Whenever the marriage is anything more than a social contract or whenever his life is not already decided, a man writes himself down at a certain value and must hang up his hunting-spears to be drawing-room ornaments. One of the chief reasons why I would be afraid of marriage in my own case is that I would be afraid my children would be like me. The thought of Stannie-like children troubles me. This is not very egotistical, is it?

In the later centuries in Europe the love of money for its own sake was held a degrading vice and the miser was a stock character in fiction. Is the miser extinct now? I think not while we have police pensioners with us. Today the love of much learning for its own sake seems to have usurped this vice without incurring the obloquy which should attach to intellectual misery.[2] Except in the mind of one. I despise these spectacled, bookish people.

Today I met with Pappie a gentleman named Clegg,[3] a solicitor who is 'down in his luck'. He had held 'very good' positions but afterwards 'lost' them. He would be a 'very clever fellow' if he 'minded his business'. He is a

2. 'Misery' in its older meaning of 'miserliness'.
3. Thomas F. Clegg.

Northerner. He told some story of a police pensioner known to both of them who had kept a public-house but was now in the Isle of Man. Clegg explained how he lived rent-free in his 'beautiful island home' and had 'a bit over', on which he comes to Dublin in the summer time, sees 'all his old friends', and goes back after a good stay here. 'What do you think of that for finance?' These stupid Northerns. Nothing stirs their admiration but the 'finance' in a man spending a shilling and getting back one-and-six.

Might-have-beens are often securer of their reputations than those who have achieved themselves.

A man is what he thinks, looks what he eats, and his manner holds up the mirror to the life he leads.

I try to avoid rudeness, for in my case rudeness is not the smaller working of a complete egoism which consistently prefers its own impulse, since it is not inconsiderateness of others' feelings because I am rationally decided in favour of my own whim, but rather a weakness, a momentary blinding of rational choice by an impulse to vent oneself, or a desire to seem something so as to overbear, or a grossness which does not see that it offends. Therefore I dislike it. I think there are occasions when by the sacrifice of an impulse of no special importance to us, we can respect the feelings of others, whose minds, though they may be inferior, even offensive, to our own, yet as civil minds deserve the civility of freedom and privacy, and the discernment of these occasions is, perhaps, a mark of refinement.

On one occasion I had a long argument with Jim about the respect for Pappie which he professes amongst strangers. I maintained that Jim's respect was false and a pure prejudice, and that as he was unable to defend it rationally, persistence in it was a lie. We were arguing quickly and Jim found himself cornered. 'Then your respect is false?' 'Yes.' 'And a prejudice?' 'Yes.' 'And when Uncle Willie told you that he hated Jack Joyce, you should not have stood up to leave?' 'No, I should not.' Having got him so far, I remarked quickly, 'You're a bloody liar,' at which Jim gave a shout of laughter. When he had finished, I proceeded to show him why I thought he should respect Pappie. I have written that I hated Pappie, that I loathed him even, but I think I have again to retract, or rather again to write down that my mind has changed. This is a poor admission after so much writing, and after so much changing I fear to write this down as final. Out on 'quod scripsi, scripsi,' and out on 'quod dixi, dixi,' too! His mind is old, and full of prejudices that are not my prejudices, and youth will have youth; his mind is opposed and abusive, and I am impatient. I am very impatient, and my just impatience has vitiated my judgment. I have not a particle of original affection for him, but just a particle of admiration for a character of vitality and a judgment which is occasionally strange and his own. Yet the greater part of what I have written about him is true, while the greater part of what I have written about myself (O stupidity!) seems false.

Pappie's own judgment of himself he rarely tells. To-night, being drunk, he mused to himself, 'I'm like the Bourbons, I never forget. I don't learn much, perhaps, but I forget very little.'

That neo-Catholic argument in favour of confession, which says that confession is a need of the human conscience and an emotional relief, is quite true, but is equally a defence of those 'Confessions' and novels which the Church discountenances as most dangerous to morals, and the second part of it equally a defence of that scortatory love in which characters of too great susceptibility, pent up by sensitiveness and reserve, find emotional relief. For my part I find the practice of confession abhorrent, though while in the Church I had neither any choice of confessors nor appreciable difficulty in telling my tale, except whatever would arise from ignorance. I see now that if I had known how to confess, I might have turned it to some end.

It is typical of me that I am more easily led to believe good of others than of myself. The Murrays say that Charlie has more consideration for Aunt Josephine and that he likes her better than I. I think they mean by considerateness an occasional forbearance with off-hand treatment, and if they do I suspect it is true that I am inconsiderate. For rudeness and slights that seem small to them, I suppose, vex me into the gut, and when they are deliberate, anger takes me by the shoulders and shakes me. Aunt Josephine tells me as a kind of reproach that she has to be far more careful in what she says or does to me than she would be with either Jim or Charlie. I feel it as a kind of reproach. Perhaps such punctiliousness seems to them arrogance affected for the purpose of overbearing, but I seem to myself to make a good effort not to be hasty, and when, having calmed my mind, the rudeness still makes its appeal to me, I would have to reproach myself with a meanness if I let the offence go by the board. If, on the other hand, it should suggest itself to them to adopt the same standard with me as I do with them (which would obviously be an affectation), I think I would supply them with very little cause. As to whether Charlie likes Aunt Josephine better than I do, I know neither how much Charlie likes her nor to what degree I like her, but just as I would trust Jim's emotion to be purer than mine, I am inclined to think that whatever feeling I have is purer than Charlie's. And so, though I didn't doubt them at the time, I think I was led to believe them too easily.

There is no happiness for the gross, who have no understanding.

When family jealousy asserts itself and there is a difference between the Murrays and ourselves, or more precisely between Uncle Willie and Pappie, I take no part. What part I do take bears witness to an impulse in me to take up Pappie's cause straightway. My conscience does not become very uneasy for its justice's sake in doing this, as Pappie is at least as trustworthy as Uncle Willie. Yet when this jealousy is at rest, I find it intolerable to remain at home with Pappie and the household. Pappie says that I flout him and that I 'declare to win' with the Murrays, so that from the first it would appear that blood is thicker than water and from the second that it is just as little preferred. I do not like Pappie for the same reason that I do not like my country, because he has surrounded me with unhappiness and opposition from my youth continually.

I have read 'The Little White Bird' of J. M. Barrie. It is the first of Barrie's I have read and is pretty like the title but not always interesting. The scheme of the book changes. Even one who, unlike me, does not first judge all things under the sun submitted to his notice and then try to frame his judgment into words, would remark this. Part of it is written for the mature mind, part of it for the child mind, and indeed his attempt at child logic is good. The mind behind the book is not strong, and from this and the conception of the book and its subject, I would have thought it was by a woman. But its delicacy would have shown me it was not, for J. M. Barrie has not only a very gentle and happy mind but—at times, in chapters, in the first and last chapters, for instance—a very graceful, delicate and pretty manner and a brilliant and mature style. There is the vice of sentimentality, of course, and the characters, while quaint and engaging, are impossible in the same way as cameos but not always so pleasing to the eye.

'The Philosophy of Pythagoras has remained,' says Walter Pater, 'in a cloud of legendary glory . . . like some antique fable richly embossed with starry wonders.' Compare with Mangan's image

> The Heavens, too, shine like a mystic book
> All bright with burning words.

Mangan wrote first. It seems to me that the charge of plagiarism is the vainest of all charges. An author should have license, I think, to make use of what has been well expressed by another, and when he borrows directly, people who detect him will be only too anxious to show their own cleverness by accusing him of dishonesty if he does not acknowledge his indebtedness. An author should be censured, I think, only when he borrows continually or where the expressions are spoiled in the borrowing. Here the plagiarism is inverse and concealed.

Jim professed a great contempt for the morality of the Irish Mystics. He said their leaving the churches was useless and nominal, for when they left them they tried to become latter-day saints. Even as such they do not compare either for consistency, holiness, or especially charity with a fifth-rate saint of the Catholic Church.

[*10 February 1904*]

Mallock[1] wrote a book called 'Is Life Worth Living'. Hasn't the title something of the naïveté of the Japanese students who hanged themselves because they could not 'make out the riddle of the Universe'? Mallock, who is not a Catholic, I believe, answers that it is not worth living outside the Catholic Church. The title is of course too big and the style is putrid. Jim wanted to know was prose worth writing. The book suggests certain difficulties as to the foundations of morals and the ideas of psychology in the philosophy of unbelievers. Amongst other things, he says of the Catholic Church that 'as the world's capacities for knowledge grow, the teacher must be always able to unfold to it a fuller teaching'. This is in fact the policy of the Church; nevertheless it would repudiate this statement of it, for this is only a euphemistic way of saying that the Church must wait on the essays and inventions of profane inquirers and adapt its teaching to them. The Church would be taught, not teacher, here, or at best an impostor of a teacher. How can I teach you more fully what you teach me? How, above all, can I interpret for you with any authority what you must first teach me? Besides, this criticism presumes a constant evolution in the Church's teach-

1. William Hurrell Mallock (1849–1923), a nephew of the Froudes. The book appeared in 1879.

ing, but as the Church claims that its teaching was given in full and as it is now to the apostles, and stakes its whole authority on this claim, and as the 'Summa' [2] it still quotes was written in the twelfth century, it cannot consign [3] to this. It is plain we must either be Mediaeval or unbelieving; the nineteenth and twentieth centuries do not believe in an anthropomorphic God or the immortality of the soul. The gulf between the Christian belief and temper and the belief and mind of the modern world is daily becoming more difficult to bridge over, and men have lost respect for that once tyrant Church which is now trying to temporize. And again, the Church has always been notoriously opposed—the phrase is mild—to those who have taught it. Witness Galileo, Columbus, Darwin. 'From this belief,' he says, 'in ourselves we shall pass to the belief in God as its only rational basis and its only emotional completion.' The belief in God is the least contested of Christian dogmas. The nature of God, the belief in the soul, the nature of the soul and its immortality—these are of far dearer importance. How much does belief in a God force one to accept? In another place he says, 'There never was a religious body except the Roman that laid the immense stress she does on all her dogmatic teaching, and had yet the justice that comes of sympathy for those that cannot receive them. The holy and humble men of heart who do not know her, or who in good faith reject her, she commits with confidence to God's uncovenanted mercies, and these she

2. *Summa de veritate catholicae fidei contra gentiles* of St. Thomas Aquinas, written in the thirteenth century, not the twelfth.

3. I.e., in the older meaning of 'subscribe'.

knows are infinite.' 'Holy and humble of heart!' Fudge. What has the Church to do with the hearts of its opponents? Who sees the heart? The first part says only that the Catholic Church is the most dogmatic, and that, considering this, it has not acted any more tyrannically than its fellows. This may or may not be true, and in either case is of little importance to a world which has lost its anxiety to be revenged. My quarrel with the second part is that it handed these good men over to God's uncovenanted mercies before their natural time. 'The God of Christianity does not make hell, still less does He deliberately put men into it. . . . God never wills the death of the sinner.' I can find no mention of hell either in the creed of the Council of Trent or in the Nicene Creed, nor any mention of Christ's descent into it. Purgatory is mentioned in the creed of the Council of Trent, and the omission of any mention of Hell can scarcely be an oversight. The Apostle's Creed says 'he descended into hell.' (By the bye, Christ is literally dead and damned. If not, out of hell there must be some redemption.) If the hell into which Christ descended was a temporary tank to hold souls, then there is no mention of hell in two Creeds. Except they get it in edgeways through this opening: 'I believe in the Holy Catholic Church.' The Church without a shadow of a doubt teaches its flock to believe in hell. If there is a hell, we are told there are people in it, and if it is as hot as they say it is, you may take your oath that men do not deliberately put themselves into it. But if they do, this fact is so contemptuous of the chaste delights of heaven that I think they ought to conceal it. There is, of course, the Irish choice, 'heaven for climate, and hell for society.'

If the effects of civilization are to be a refinement of

our species and liberality and culture and moral freedom, then I can quite understand why Goethe regretted Martin Luther's influence on his countrymen. Martin Luther seems to have been a man of turbulent and passionate but doggedly courageous temper. He is blunt and impatient in intellect, setting no value on philosophy (indeed I am not sure that he did not regard it as one of the Devil's false sciences) and has credulous prejudices worthy of a miner's son. I have always been given to believe that there was a protestant, anti-catholic falsity in both Luther's admiration and abuse, but I find it consistent with my idea of him to believe that at a time of ecclesiastical rottenness and, in himself, of unbelief and hardly restrained rebelliousness, he was taken by a sincere admiration of the Bible and by the idea of deliberate differences between it and the teaching of the Church of which he was a priest, and that, gradually making this his standard of battle, he added thereto the impeachment of the lives of the religious of his time, yet I suspect he did not add this to his charge till he had made his own life conformable to Christian ethics. He founds a religion by making a schism, for his courage is timid at first till he numbers his followers, and makes a schism by opposing corrupt practices. The stand he takes, and he says that at first he stood alone, is scarcely at all theological, for he is no theologian though a doctor of the Church, in fact he never claims to be one and even admits that his declaration of belief was drawn up by Melanchthon, and as a scholar he is not noteworthy. He is certainly no philosopher; he seems almost ignorant. In support of the very roots of his creed he cites the silliest tags of arguments; and his opinions on nearly all questions are almost absolutely worthless, and show a narrow-minded prejudice scarcely less intolerable than that he wished to overthrow. It must be admitted that in any argument on the celibacy of the clergy it is philosophically unsatisfying to say that if a priest finds it very difficult to remain chaste and lead an exemplary life, he should marry. Luther calls marriage a 'plaster for the sore'. The Bible, too, he treats as churls treat that they love, rejecting as foolish in it whatever he does not understand. His cry seems to be against ceremony and elaborate doctrine in the Church, and hypocrisy and tyrannical government in ecclesiastics. I think that it is safe to say that the great part of Europe which once accepted him as its leader has fallen away from him and forgotten all but his name. But his name remains a banner of revolt.

Luther, for a name that begins an age of dispute and revolution and bloodshed and a double religious persecution, stands for very little in the way of advance on feudalism or new and timely spiritual impulse. I dislike Lutheranism from what I know of it, its stolid, narrow piety and its wooden rigorous morality, a bourgomaster's religion, mere sociology with belief in a redeemer and a managing God to justify its title of religion at all, yet for Germany he did one good work. He claims respect as a German patriot, almost as a European patriot, because it was by him that a powerful Italian Government was broken in Germany, and in many countries following Germany in Europe.

He is simple and honest; but honesty is such a plebeian virtue, and perhaps means no more than the lack of the wit to deceive. There is a kind of rusticity rather than simplicity in his tale of the false vision of Jesus crucified on Good Friday, and I admire an honesty rarely found in preachers and religious reformers in his confession that he expects greater goodness from Kate, his wife, from Melanchthon, and from other friends, than from his sweet and blessed Saviour Jesus Christ. That Jesus is not present to him his remarks would shew, he as much as admits that he lives rather as a name than as a personality for him, and, recognizing what if it were in relation to a simple man or woman he would call a falsity in his love of Jesus, he blames a weakness in human nature. Blame rather an impossibility in the thing demanded itself. He is a good type, above all, of that commonplace pessimism which comes to us when we begin to learn the extent of the ills of the body—'How many sorts of death are there in our bodies?' says he—and of the vices of the body and mind, and how we have the germs of them all in ourselves, that pessimism which more than awe or reason establishes religion in the vulgar. He never tires of reiterating that 'the imagination of man's heart is evil from his youth, and the thoughts of his heart evil continually.' 'How should God deal with us?' he cries. 'Good days we cannot bear, evil we cannot endure. Gives he riches unto us? Then we are proud so that no man can live by us in peace; nay, we will be carried upon heads and shoulders, and will be adored as Gods. Gives he poverty unto us? Then are we dismayed and impatient and murmur against him. Therefore nothing were better for us than forthwith to be covered over with the shovel.'

It is part of the overbearing policy of the Catholic Church to give its too docile children to believe that Protestantism has no belief, but is a self-confounding label. I find it very hard to discover from Luther what religion he interpreted to his followers, his discourses are so little theological; in fact I find very little more definite instructions than 'to believe in Jesus Christ who died for us'. In his bluntness he gives utterance to the attitude of the only Christian Church till then towards unbelievers, an attitude that had been left unexpressed till then from policy. 'With him,' says Luther, 'who admits the authority of Christ and the Gospel are we ready to dispute, but with him who denies these we will hold no parley.' What I gather to be the chief tenet of that 'rotten and unsound doctrine which would save only those that lived at Wittenberg', is that the passion and death of Jesus, the son of God, were all sufficient for the salvation of mankind and that we are saved by faith only, that we should believe simply what we know of Christ, in his love for us, and try to keep his law, and he in his mercy will do the rest. He discourages inquiry into the reasons for this belief rather funnily, telling how Saul's sin was that he believed in God's law as the highest and most precious treasure and was prepared to venture even his life for it, but he sought the understanding of the law too earnestly, asking testimony of Christ from the Scribes and therefore he was banged on the ear. When I was at Belvedere I noted down many questions and objections which occurred to me in reading the catechism of a Church in which I already disbelieved, and I find amongst them this question also: Why, if the Son of God was so dear in the sight of his Father that his mere becoming man—that humiliation—was enough according to some senile injustice in His Father to appease him for the sin of our first Parents, firstly, he chose to be tortured and spat upon (though that indignity was comparatively trifling, being infinitely less than the humiliation of the Incarnation and therefore of most trivial importance; Christians, I imagine, think that it was necessary for him to be tortured; if his tortures were voluntary and unnecessary how can we have compassion for them?); secondly, why he did not cleanse the effects as well as the guilt of original sin, namely, strengthen our will, enlighten our understanding and renew in us a strong inclination to good; and thirdly, why in spite of the more than difficulty of keeping his law or His Father's he left it necessary for us to atone so bitterly for our sins? What Luther teaches about sin it is difficult, again, to make out. He rehearses the distinction made by the Schoolmen between original and actual sin, saying that original sin is the desire, the lust, the coveting—bad in itself—and leads to actual sin. Thus, he says, all inclinations are either without God or against him, as no man, for instance, would be so virtuous as to marry a wife only to have children and to bring them up in the fear of God. But God bears with them and lets them pass in such as believe in Christ. It seems to me there is more to interest one in a phrase or a passage in the Schoolmen than in all of Luther I know—though Erasmus thought differently. He says that sins are not forgiven us because we are sorry for them, for this is a natural consequence of sin itself, but because God is merciful and forgives us for Christ's sake. Neither do we fall from grace by reason of our sins, yet he reproves Schenck [4] for preaching that all sinners will be received, saying that only those will be received who have repented.

There is nothing that interests me or that I like in this turbulent priest, for he contemns what I admire, philosophy, and his spiritual nature seems to have a certain gross-

4. Jacob Schenck (fl. 1534), the Freiburg Reformer.

ness, a certain stupidity not altogether unlovely. His portrait was on the frontispiece to the only book of his I have read, his grotesquely miraculously preserved [5] 'Table-Talk'. The face is characteristic, the face of a narrow, illiberal, ignorant Parish Priest, though with a courage, and lively faith, an intensity that is not in those bestial features. I am sure he must have been an intolerable person for anyone of refined sensibility to live with, by reason of coarse manners, that his religious instructions to his children were made convincing by floggings and bangs on the ear, and that he was an impossible person to argue with.

[18 July 1904]

Monday, 18 July 1904.[1] I'm an unlucky, bloody, bloody, bloody fool. Och! I can't curse big enough! I wanted to go to this Regatta with Katsy tomorrow, I wanted to go! Curse on this ankle of mine! Curse on it! But maybe it'll be well in the morning? No, I know the kind it'll be; I'll suffer hell getting it into my boot. Oh, Jesus! I can't get my boot off! It feels like as if I was smashing my foot off at the ankle. That's only imagination I know, but if I force the boot off I may injure my foot still more by straining it, and I won't be able to put a foot under me at all tomorrow. I wanted

5. See 'Captain Henry Bell's Narrative' in the Introduction of *The Table Talk of Martin Luther*, tr. and ed. William Hazlitt (London: Bell and Daldy, 1872). Bell maintained that the copy he found buried in Germany in 1626 was the sole copy to escape destruction.

1. The following literary exercise is worked up from the incident mentioned under date of 1 August [1904]. See p. 45.

particularly to go to that cursed Regatta with Katsy. I'd have been able to borrow a shilling from Pappie; I don't often borrow, and besides, I'd have been able to pay it back—. Oh, if only I hadn't jumped at that ditch I'd have been all right now and could have gone as I intended to-morrow. Even if I do go, I'll be limping damnably about, unable to enjoy anything. Probably injuring my foot by walking on it, too. I don't care a curse. I want to go and I'll go. S-s-sis! I can't even press my foot on the floor; it strains my whole leg. I'm sick into the bargain, this thing has made me sick. I can't get this boot off, that's all about it; somebody else will have to take it off. See, I'm all trembling. I wish I had a light; this room of mine is so dark. I'll call Charlie? No, somehow I would dislike to ask him to do the least thing for me; I suppose I must dislike him. Poppie then, or Eileen? Oh, I forgot; they're down at Fairview, out with the Murrays and Katsy, while I'm here. In any case I hate to have anyone attending on me. It seems to me peevish and weak. There! It's off, that wasn't so hard. My foot seems to be singing a song, a stinking, painful song, but! I'll be into bed in a minute now—. The pain isn't so intense, but the darkness here! the uncomfortable-ness of the bed! my unluckiness—I hate to be invalided up. Boys are shouting out there behind in Cabra Park, it can't be so late, about 9 I suppose. Everyone is up and out this fine summer evening, but here am I. I suppose they're out at Donnycarny now, Katsy too. I think she prefers to be out with them than with me. They bore me utterly. I would like to run away down a side road by myself. Why does she prefer them? How long will they be; till half past ten. An hour and a half. It'll seem hours to me, the length of a night. I can't sleep on this side, I am uncomfortable. I won't be able to turn, either. It'll strain my foot. Then I'll have to lie in this one position all night. Some one of those dull, feat-performing saints remained in the one position for a week before he died, or maybe it was a month? Aye, or a year or two, perhaps? See if I can control myself, too. I'll try to abstract myself, I'll think about something. What'll I think about—? What's this I was—? Genius. Well, Genius! What's this everybody said about Genius? Carlyle said that

[Pagination of the MS shows six pages lacking here, but the context seems to give no evidence of such a lacuna.]

body subjugates and tortures the mind with pain, and the mind flies from pain as the ball flies round the hand that holds it by a string—. How long? How long will this keep on? How stupid of me to forget about that genius, because it was good—clever—. Ah, sure in any case it'll be thrown up on the scum of my mind again at some other time—'like scum' I mean, of course—. This bed is very warm now—. The skin seems tightening around my head—slowly!—slow-ly!—. Oh!—that was clever—wish I had said that—. 'A—a—a—ah—multitude'—M—said that—. What was his name?—I just caught the name, just!—Who's this said that?—Who's this?—I can't—What's this the thing was?—I can't think—remember—Dawn!—A—ah!—sink!—'A—a—a—ah multitude'—multitude—ude————. And so, sleep.[2]

2. This paragraph is one of several possible sources for James's use of the interior monologue. Referring to that use, Stanislaus on 7 August 1924 wrote to his brother: "Another point regarding your cinematographic psychological analysis. It is often obscure and it should not be so. Thought may be inconsequent, desultory, het-

I feel ungrateful when others whom I do not like, like me, because I know I will repay them with indifference if not with dislike. Pappie has lately made a difference in his manner towards Charlie and towards myself, and this troubles me. I ask myself would it not be honester for me to make him dislike me beyond the shadow of a doubt. I would prefer it to be so, for I am happier, happier, happier, freer, and better without his liking. I do not like his liking. Yet I argue this way with myself, that Pappie does not really like me (the idea is repugnant), for when I come in, the daily, fatiguing, scurrilous, endless rigamarole begins. 'Begins'—no, changes theme and key. I say nothing, grimly.[3] Then after some time he begins to tell something

---

erogeneous—anything you like—but never obscure to the thinker. How could it be so? Yet in 'Ulysses', Bloom's wool-gatherings as often as not leave the reader guessing. This is a mistake, in my opinion and vitiates the whole book. I have the right, I think, to make this observation as, of the two, I first attempted to write out the rambling thoughts—and of a person lying awake in bed, too— until he fell asleep. This in my diary, under the date of Monday, the 18th July 1904, I still have. You chucked it aside with a contemptuous phrase: 'the youthful Maupassant'. At that time you were writing, to my entire satisfaction, about 'the faith that in the Middle Ages sent the spires singing up to Heaven'. You were wrong. No writer so artificial as Maupassant suggested it to me. It was the description of the death of a Russian lieutenant in Tolstoy's story 'Sebastopol' that gave me the idea. I had forgotten the lieutenant's name because I have not seen the book since then. You need not grudge me these small claims. After all, the hint, to which I myself attached no importance at the time, is nothing. The work is all" (*Letters of James Joyce*, ed. Ellmann, II, 103–104).

3. MS note: 'I know it is not because I am twenty and idle, for it has been going on since I can remember.'

that has happened through the day and in which I take not the least interest. The abusiveness has gone out of his words, but not yet out of his tone and manner. I allow myself to answer him, even to talk about what does not interest me, though I am aware that disgust, like Katsy, glances at my eyes, and silently does not admire. I see that he wants someone to talk to. Why should I not talk to him while I am here? And then this happens. I am down in Murrays. Aunt Josephine being ill, I have called to see her. Uncle Willie comes in unexpectedly, and after a few minutes I get up to go. I am asked to stay. I make some efforts to go, but being pressed both by Uncle Willie and Aunt Josephine, and being undecided, I stay against my better judgment. It is the first time for I don't know how long that I have stayed the evening. You might have been more careful than to have left it possible; you compromised your self-respect for no visible purpose. Uncle Willie in the middle of a drunken, rambling, apparently friendly speech to me aimed covert insults at Jim and, in a lower tone to Aunt Josephine, open insults. Katsy had asked me to wait until she returned from the chapel, and when she came in, having played a few short games of cards, I left. I was annoyed as usual with myself for having put myself in the way of a vulgar jealousy which I know so well. Pappie was drunk when I came home. He is under the impression that every night that I am late, I have been down with them. 'Oh, ye bloody-looking Yahoo of hell! Down with the Murrays were ye?' 'Is my supper ready, please?' 'How long, Oh Jesus, how long? Oh wait! A fortnight! Just about a fortnight and then I'll pelt the Murrays with you. Pelt them, by God.' Then he proceeded to tell how Tom

Devon [4] asked what Charlie and I were doing, and how he told Devon he was going to put us on the street when he sold the house. 'And what are they going to do?' 'Oh, they tell me they can go down and stay with the Murrays. Willie Murray will take them in; in fact, I believe he's very anxious for them to go down! Oh yes, and chat'll travel.' He said much more that was equally offensive, but the text of his discourse I know to be true, that Uncle Willie has no love for Jim or for me or for anyone of our name. I listened tiredly to him for some time. What had been wearisomely wrong for months was wearisomely true tonight. I thought of it on the way home. He might have been present, and yet in spite of his drunkenness he is not without impartiality, as if he were exercising his mind really to tell me that which is. My scanty respect for him is relative, not absolute. Ugh! How much I write about this family bickering, but then, how much it thrusts itself upon me! However, Aunt Josephine is not Uncle Willie, and I am not my father. Aunt Josephine alluded to the phrase that occurs so often in these 'Notes'—'the Murrays'. I have grown up with it; it [is] associated in my mind forever with the sound of Pappie's voice drunkenly haranguing his silent family, that deep, open-vowelled, rasping, blatant voice, listening to which, at least I understand hate.

In all these interminable controversies between unbelievers and the churches and their different creeds, what are their arguments from? Certainly—certain premises? I think not, but from probability; a mundane logical shrewdness guides them. The effect of the reading of religious eristic writing is to make me feel lecherously disposed. I un-

4. Devin.

derstand Boccaccio and his school then. The churches say 'there is no continence except in Thee, O Lord.' It is, perhaps, desirable that they were right.

My mind used to have a very disputatious turn when I was younger. I used to take up some opinion that pleased me and in my mind argue with some figmentary opponent something in this way:—Concerning the idea of education. —See, there is a man going alone along the Malahide Rd. Supposing he has nothing great on his mind, he is not a lover, nor in the expectation of plenty like the farmer that hanged himself, supposing he has no great trouble, his only child has not died, he has not lost all his money, supposing, too, he is not a philosopher, what is he thinking about? Nothing, you say. But how does one decide, how do I decide what is the probable right answer? I cast about in my memory to try if I can find there what I think about in similar circumstances. Then it seems to me that only in a dreamless sleep is there nothing in the living mind. If you still persist for argument sake in holding that there is nothing in his mind, I think I can convince you this way. His eyes are open, and if he is not blind he sees. Yes, he sees, you say but his mind is silent. But listen. If you hold a glass before the scene he is passing, will it not reflect it more truly than the retina of his eye? Does the glass, then, 'see'? Seeing implies consciousness, and you cannot in seriousness pretend to doubt, with that tag of scepticism, that the glass is not conscious, for we believe for reasons almost innumerable that it is not, for the reasons for instance that men by taking thought have made it what it is, a glass, and as it was made, just so it remains, nor does it ever move itself, nor reflect things in the manner it chooses, but as they are presented to it, nor reflect only such things as it chooses, nor has it showed any signs that are even of life, neither grew nor was capable of growth, reproduced nor was capable of reproducing. But the mind 'sees', that is, is conscious of the image the eye reflects for it, and says continually within itself: 'This is a road, the Malahide Rd. I know it well now that I see it. There are high broken hedges on both sides of it, and a few trees. Where the road branches, an irregular dwelling-house with an orchard about it sidles to an arm, and before, parting the bifurcation, is an old gate entrance. There is a young fellow on the opposite side going in the same direction as I am': thinking not in sentences as in a book, but thought succeeding thought without utterance, like harmonies in music, while conveying a more definite impression to the mind. So much for what is in his mind. Now it seems to me that the right purpose of education is to make these impressions and thoughts and judgments distinct, intelligible, and definite. Such an education, you say, would make a man very silent and self-centred. It would, to a certain degree, but in that succession of thoughts there would come impressions that would be beautiful and imaginative, original or witty or brilliant thoughts that would not be kept silent, and judgments that would remain as precious things kept bravely in the mind, that, linking wit and brilliancy and imagination, would influence a mind seeing beauty and remembering happiness, would refine and mould it to a free and potent nobility.— Such thinking seems to me vain and vulgar, as if I were showing off to a spectator also figmentary. It seems vulgar because except the last it was thought easily and with a secret distrust of its logic and yet passed. It would have been better to spend time and call the eye, for instance, a conscious glass. It is stupid, too, for I make my interlocutor stupid to make an argument in the first place, and then the easier to beat him down. Uncle Willie said to me 'you with your Socratic mind'. He didn't believe himself, or reserved the right not to believe himself, and to think his own mind better than Socratic; but he was right in a way. There is something feebly Socratic in its style. I like my leisure and can use it, my mind gives me ordinary fare for pleasure, but how cumbrously my brain works in its shell. I see the road I go plainly, the bare hedges and trees and lush Spring colours, but I do not see one step before or after. But for the light of the conscious glass my mind is dark. How many are like me?

I am considered hardier and healthier than either Jim or Charlie. I take care of myself and watch my body almost as carefully as I watch my mind, but I seem to myself to have been braving off weakness and delicacy always and in all respects. I regard myself as one of the naturally weak.

How men idle is a better test of their quality than what they work at. It always seemed to me that almost all men became commonplace when they set to work . . . to 'transact business'. Their work is at best a test of their proper aptitude and abilities, and even very rarely a test of this. Their relaxation, too, is placed through their energies in inverse ratio to their abilities. A Prime Minister diverts himself for weeks by hitting a ball over golf links. But on their idleness men leave fuller imprints of their minds.

I need to develop my memory to give myself a grip on my thoughts.

From here, under a sane evening, infinitely high and

spacious, a dry white road narrows and slopes over the bent of the hill and appears narrower still away down there where, between pretty red terraces, it enters the utmost rim of the city with its lines of houses and chimney tops. The tiny figures of human beings seem like pen-marks on a picture. The sun, a flaming shield of silver gold, has gone down behind a low bank of clouds, shooting shafts of light. A cold stir is the breeze. A blast from the arch-angel's trumpet would blaze out from this hill over the city only to fall spent out and hang like a vapour over the coldly rippled sea beyond. . . . My walk leads me round by a monastery gate and where over hilly fields the shades of evening are deepening grass green, and hidden birds quietly chirrup separately. That emptiness from the hill has made me feel petty and useless and isolated in this crowded world. What life, be it ever so generous or fine, can be more than a tiny pen-mark? Yet it would be mon-strous for any human thing or image to fill that vast empti-ness. My walk is a round put in till it is time to go home to tea in the bare parlour in Cabra, red and warm in the light of the fire and the lamp. How can that please me, except under protest, for that vast unfilled evening is an-other quiet, permanent reproach?

The Jesuit influence, not their system, is educational, because it trains those under it to educate themselves.

A reply to a matrimonial advertisement: 'Undersigned begs to apply for above position.'

Matter is indestructible, scientists tell us, so here is an epitaph for mortalists: 'Here lie the immortal remains.'

I was in the prettily-furnished, softly-carpeted house of a Belfast builder today. Every cheap luxury a clerk could want was there in some corner. There was everything—except room. His wife appeared to be cooking the dinner in the kitchen. His children's children will shiver at the space between sky and sea. I know poverty, yet I prefer our house with its dirty windows and door and without even the necessary furniture, because, perhaps for this reason, there is no shameful want of room, and I understand Diogenes' preference for poverty.

I prefer either music or prose to verse, but I like poetry wherever it is found. I admit it is found oftenest in verse.

I have so much sympathy with people I know that when I am in the same room with them and silent, everything that happens them seems to happen me and I pass through every mood of theirs. How can I believe, then, that I have a mind of my own. Add to this that I have no affection for my family, and I will show something strange. I am silent and reserved to live with for this reason, that I wish my conversation with those who expect affection from me but to whom I can offer none, to be civil, what is necessary, but no more. I would prefer to live with strangers, because I do not succeed as I wish in my attempt. But I watch over myself with irritable scrupulousness lest a tone, a superfluous word, a look, a spontaneous expression might be misunderstood. I have defined love as an intimate and desirous dependence. Isn't this the opposite of that love—an intimate but repugnant dependence—and do I, then, hate all my family who tacitly expect affection from me?

I have a novel system of reading: I sell what books I can, and read what books I can't—out of spite.

I attribute the following to Pappie: (1) the undermining of his children's health, and their rotting teeth, to absolutely irregular feeding and living, cheap adulterated food, and general unsanitary conditions of life; (2) the handicap of his children's chances in life (whereby Poppie's chance, for example, is quite ruined); (3) Mother's unhealth, unhappiness, weakening mind, and death, to his moral brutality and the Juggernaut he made life with him, and to his execrable treatment of her even up to her last day; and (4), indirectly, Georgie's death, for if Georgie had been properly doctored or in a hospital, he would have lived. Besides these, he is pulling down his children's characters with him as he sinks lower. It's a pretty list on paper yet somewhat understated. 'Moral brutality' does not convey to the stranger mind the eternity of abuse that in memory impinges monotonously on my accustomed ear at will. It was a constant threat of his to Mother, 'I'll break your heart! I'll break your bloody heart!' It must be admitted that this was exactly what he did, but not of set purpose. He saw that his callous habit of commonplace gluttony, as graceless and dull a routine as the rest of his life, would have this effect, and it eased his ill nature to think so. He uses the threat to us, now, but adds, 'I'll break your stomach first though, ye buggers. You'll get the effects of it later on. Wait till you're thirty and you'll see where you'll be.' He has made the house what it has always been by his unlovely nature and his excellent appetite for whiskey and water, and that he has any pension left to live upon is due to the influence of friends and consideration for the family dependent on him. He was near being left without. Here is one out of my Book of Days. On Thursday the 27th April,[5] I was up fairly early—8 perhaps—

5. 1902.

and the day went according to my plan till a certain hour. Pappie was defendant in an appeal case and expected the case to be called. He was going to defend the action himself. I went down to see. I did not see, for it was not called, and I came home at six. Pappie was not in, there was no light, and no meal. I had wasted my day waiting for him in the Four Courts—a snobbish, utterly stupid, noisy hole—while he was getting drunk in some bar parlour or snug. I was irritated, for I knew he had money. I sat down heavily on the table and cursed his name vehemently. Poppie, who had been moping over the fire in the dark with the children, began to ease her own irritation and her tongue on me. I cursed at her like Pappie's son and went out. I was happy out—but what to do in such a house? Answer advertisements? Is anything more futile and disheartening? And what to do out? Aunt Josephine was laid up, so they would not be out, and my customary relief was blocked. I walked out to Dollymount by myself, then I came home, after nine. Pappie was not in yet. I had been speculating by outward signs about it while I knocked and had given myself hope. I cursed again violently for perhaps a minute, and was silent. Afterwards I went up to bed. It was partly stomach anger, it was partly a fanning of resentment into violent hatred, but it was deep irritation at myself far more than these. For some idea of amiability I had lived with him for some days and had consented not [to] go with those my thoughts should have chosen. Lâche! I had acted the part of companion to him—'acted' is the word, for I knew that my slight, perceptible dislike for him was as constant and unchanging as my slight, perceptible pity for Mother. I felt my pride outwitted and humiliated.

After ten Pappie came in with few pence left. We—and the children—had fasted 14 hours. I heard his drunken intonations in the dark downstairs, and then the saddening flow. This is a true portrait of my progenitor: the leading one a dance and then the disappointing, baffling, baulking and turning up drunk—the business of breaking hearts.

Postscript

The latest date mentioned in the diary is January 1905. In October of that year, at James's invitation, Stanislaus left Dublin and joined his brother in Trieste. He took a job teaching English at the Berlitz School and immediately placed his salary, and even his extra trousers, at the disposal of his fellow tutor James. Stanislaus proved himself to be a conscientious and diligent teacher and for the next ten years became his brother's keeper. His brother never needed him more. James was disheartened by publishers, annoyed at the new responsibilities of fatherhood, temporarily bored by Nora, depressed by the frustrations of authorship, and too easily disposed to escape his unhappiness in bars. Stanislaus sustained him resolutely, but the business was so distasteful that he once thought of clearing out and returning to Dublin. But he did not go back, then or ever.

In January 1915, because of the war, Stanislaus as a British subject was arrested and forced to spend the war years in detention centers. James, equally alien but as usual luckier, was allowed with his family to leave Austrian territory for Switzerland, where he spent those years writing *Ulysses.* When peace returned, the brothers were reunited in Trieste but discovered that their relations with one another had cooled. James had found new friends and keepers and no longer so much needed his brother. Stanislaus on his part had lost considerable confidence in his brother's genius because of *Ulysses,* much of which he then thought unintelligible. As the brothers continued to drift apart, James in 1920 left Trieste for Paris and the coming years of public acclaim. Stanislaus remained where he was and received a professorship of English, once held by James, at the University of Trieste. The old warm relationship between the brothers was never entirely renewed.

In 1927 Stanislaus married an attractive university student, Nelly Lichtensteiger, and for a while lived quietly as a successful teacher and husband. But in 1936 his detestation of Mussolini brought about the loss of his professorship and an order for his deportation. These troubles passed, however, and after a brief sojourn in Switzerland he returned to Trieste and his old position. There were rare visits to James but old times refused to renew themselves. James was deep in the fascination of *Finnegans Wake:* Stanislaus dismissed that work as "witless wandering" and "drivelling rigamarolle." James found sufficient satisfaction in his Paris circle, and Stanislaus was content with his ordered life in Trieste. They never again quite stood shoulder to shoulder. Still, the last note Joyce wrote before his death in 1941 was to Stannie, and Stannie, deeply grieved after the loss of his brother, took up his role as defender of the James he had known and revered. Though Stanislaus again suffered discomfort during the second war

—he was still technically a British subject—he must have been cheered by the birth in February 1943 of his and Nelly's only child. He named his son James.

Stanislaus, born in Dublin on 17 December 1884, died in Trieste at the age of seventy on 16 June 1955. It was Bloomsday.

Index

Tinayre, Marcelle, 65 n.
Tolstoy, Leo, 133, 145, 168 n.
Touchett, Ralph (character), 122
Trent, Council of, 159
Trieste, 179, 180, 181
Turgenev (Tourgeniev, Turgenieff, Turgeniev), I. S., 62, 85, 133
Tyndall, John, 57

Ulysses, 8 n., 13 n., 14 n., 21 n., 45 n., 61 n., 65 n., 78 n., 82 n., 104 n., 168 n., 180
United Irishman, 97 n.
University College, Dublin, 95, 148n.

Velasquez, 24, 78
Verdon, Rev. John T., 106 n.
Vernon, Fr., 106
Voltaire, 103

Wagner, Richard, 146

Waldteufel, Emile, 147
Walker, Marie, 35
Warburton, Lord (character), 121
Werther, 127
"What counsel has the learned moon," 24 n.
White, traveler, 81
Whitford, Vernon (character), 121, 128
Whitman, Walt, 79
Whitworth Hospital, 43
Wilde, Oscar, 21
Wilhelm Meister, 127
Winterbourne (character), 123, 127, 128, 131

Yeats, Jack B., 107
Yeats, W. B., 25, 26, 63, 117
Yggdrasill, 3
Young Irelanders, 26

Zola, Emile, 82

The Complete Dublin Diary
of Stanislaus Joyce

Designed by R. E. Rosenbaum.
Composed by Vail-Ballou Press, Inc.
in 11 point linotype Janson, 3 points leaded,
with display lines in monotype Caslon Old Style 337.
Printed letterpress from type by Vail-Ballou Press
on Warren's 1854 text, 60 lb. basis,
with the Cornell University Press watermark.
Bound by Vail-Ballou Press
in Interlaken Pallium bookcloth,
and stamped in black foil and genuine gold.